From a Pheasant Hunter's Notebook

FROM A
Pheasant Hunter's Notebook

LARRY BROWN

Iowa State University Press / Ames

Larry Brown is an outdoor writer, currently Iowa editor of *Outdoor Life* magazine.

© 1992 Iowa State University Press, Ames, Iowa 50010

⊗ Printed on acid-free paper in the United States of America

First edition, 1992

Some of the photographs in this book have appeared in *Iowa Game and Fish, Modern Pheasant Hunting, Fins and Feathers, The American Hunter,* and *The Drummer.*

Library of Congress Cataloging-in-Publication Data

Brown, Larry.
    From a pheasant hunter's notebook / Larry Brown.—1st ed.
       p. cm.
    Includes bibliographical references.
    ISBN 0-8138-0498-1.—ISBN 0-8138-0492-2 (pbk.)
    1. Pheasant shooting. I. Title.
  SK325.P5B76 1992
  799.2′48617—dc20   91-13829

TO MY FATHER,

who first put a gun in my hands
and taught me how to hunt,
and to all the companions,
human and canine,
with whom I've since enjoyed
good times afield.

CONTENTS

FOREWORD

The phone rang last night about nine o'clock. I wasn't surprised to hear Larry Brown's voice; after all, Iowa's pheasant hunting season had just ended.

"You should have come out," Larry said. "It was a good year."

"How good?"

"I ended with sixty-three. That's the best I've ever done, and I lost a couple of weeks at the end of the season when I was in Washington on active duty."

Larry is a lieutenant colonel in the Army Reserve. Usually, he doesn't let Uncle Sam tamper with his pheasant hunting.

"I feel sorry for you," I said. "Gee, only sixty-three roosters."

My friend does this to me every year. Larry doesn't boast. He knows only too well how much this rooster-hungry Michigan hunter also enjoys chasing Hawkeye State ringnecks. I pick my shots for Brown, too, equally roasting him when he misses out on grouse or woodcock hunting at home with me.

I met Larry Brown in Milwaukee in July of 1979 at a meeting of state editors for *Fins and Feathers* magazine. He invited several of us to come to Iowa for pheasant hunting that fall. Larry mesmerized us with glowing talk about sloughs stiff with corn-fed ringnecks. Fencerow point after point. The excellent possibility of shooting a true double. You could hear the passion in Larry's voice and see it on his face and in his animation.

This man loves pheasants, I remember thinking.

He still does. That is why it is so much fun to hunt with him and why those postseason phone calls get to me so easily.

During the past ten years, I cannot recall a single pheasant hunt in Iowa without being in the company of Larry Brown. Over that span of time, a man who hunts can build up quite a portfolio of experience. The Thanksgiving Day thunderstorm that drove us

ix

from the field when we realized that our guns were perfect lightning rods. Sun-drenched sloughs on an Amish farm. Chisel-plowed corn ground on another farm, the black clods of earth shining like anthracite. On a third, the gumbo earth that clung to our boots like black cement.

Sometimes Gene or Steve or Mike or Dave hunted with us. Or Larry's friends from college, where he teaches French: Denny, Todd, Neil. The November day my son, Brian, pricked the carpet-tack spurs on his first ringneck. Three of us shamefully missed that bird before Brian downed it with a 20 gauge single-shot. And the dogs—my Brinka, Macbeth, Chaucer, and Holly; and Larry's own Irish Nick (the red rocket) and pointers Jake and Rebel and Heidi; and the others, like Brandy and Briar and Pepper.

Wonderful experiences all. We slept in motels, motor homes, and farmhouse bedrooms. We ate in truck stops, Amana Colony restaurants, farm kitchens, and a dozen or more no-name cafes and taverns like the one in Amber where a mounted whitetail buck watched us with his dust-covered eyes while we ate huge buck-apiece hamburgers.

Over a period of ten years, you learn a lot about a man who chooses to hunt with you. You learn to take your own birds because Larry won't contribute to *your* limit when his is satisfied. You learn to unload the gun promptly at 4:30 each afternoon, the end of legal shooting time in Iowa, even when the pointer has a certain rooster nailed in the switchgrass. You hunt hard for every lost bird, and then you learn to hunt some more. You remember never to pour motel drinks until the dogs are toweled off and fed, the birds dressed, the guns wiped dry and swabbed.

If you are tied up on the phone to home, you will discover that Larry will do these chores for you.

You learn not to criticize another man, even if he takes a bird from over your gun barrel. I did that one fall to Larry in Mahaska County. His comment, "I hope I'm being a good host," made me want to sink out of sight in the gumbo we were slogging through.

You learn not to bad-mouth another man's dogs—even when they bite you, pee on you, and run over your rock-steady pointer. My charges have done all of these things, and more, to Larry.

You learn a lot about pheasant behavior and how, when, and where to best hunt these incredibly cagey birds. Brown is a rooster tactician—maybe it is his military training (he is also a former CIA agent)—with an ever-evolving game plan to match their uncanny survival skills. The perpetual student of ringneck ways, at the end of every hunting day, Larry writes in his notebook. He jots down things like hunting and weather conditions, how the birds acted, and what went right or wrong with the hunt.

He has filled many notebooks since I began hunting with him, but the daily habit goes back long before 1979.

"Why do you take so many notes?" I asked him once.

"Maybe someday I'll write a book about pheasant hunting," he said. "You never know."

This is that book. I know you will enjoy it.

Lansing, Michigan   TOM HUGGLER

PREFACE

This is a book about pheasant hunting. I assume that you are considering reading it because you are a pheasant hunter. Perhaps it was given to you as a gift, or perhaps you are thinking about buying it. In either case, you deserve to know exactly what kind of book it is, and what kind of book it isn't.

I am a native Iowan, having lived in this state 40 of my 45 years. Although I've hunted grouse and woodcock in Michigan on several occasions, and quail in North Carolina, Georgia, Kansas, and Arizona, I've only made one brief pheasant hunting trip—to South Dakota—outside of my home state.

Tom Huggler, my good friend and fellow bird hunting fanatic who was kind enough to write the foreword to this book, hunted every species of quail in the United States in a single season. That experience formed the basis for his book, *Quail Hunting in America*. Tom lives in Michigan where there are plenty of grouse and woodcock but not many quail. He couldn't have written his book without making that season-long bird hunting odyssey.

I approached this book from a very different starting point. Although I'd like to have the experience of shooting pheasants everywhere from upstate New York to the Pacific Northwest, and all the places in between where they are legal game, I have difficulty dragging myself out of Iowa during our two month plus pheasant season. I shoot grouse and woodcock before the pheasant season opens, and quail after it closes. During the season, I shoot pheasants almost exclusively, unless I happen to find myself in an area where there are also quail or Hungarian partridge. But in any case, the ringneck is my primary target.

I won't presume to tell you how to hunt pheasants in places I've never been, where there are types of cover I've never seen in Iowa. What I will try to relate to you are the experiences I've had during a lifetime of hunting in one of the best pheasant areas in the country. My pheasant hunting memories go back nearly four decades. Since 1973, I've systematically recorded those experiences, from every hunt I've made, in a series of notebooks. Thus the title of this book.

I think the word "expert" is overused to the point of being almost meaningless. I like the old line which defines an expert as someone with a slide projector and a lecture who's more than 50 miles from home. Because of where I live, what I do for a living, and my passion for pheasant hunting, I'm fortunate enough to have more experience with the birds than most people. I don't think that makes me an expert. I've hunted with some people who are more experienced than I am and many who are less experienced. I've found that I've been able to learn things from both groups.

I'm not a champion at sporting clays, skeet, or trap. I'm one of those unfortunate people who are born cross-dominant—right-handed with a left master eye. That factor, and my below average hand-eye coordination, don't exactly make me a natural deadeye. With a fair amount of practice on clay birds, and relatively frequent opportunities to look at ringnecks down the rib of a double-barrel, I've become an adequate shot. I wish that I were better. Many of you probably are.

Nor can I attribute any championship honors to my dogs. I have hunted at least three seasons with each of five different dogs, representing four different breeds. I rank two of them as very good pheasant dogs, one as well above average, one as average, and one as a total disaster. Although I'd be content to hunt for the rest of my days with canines the caliber of my two best dogs, I'm certain that some of you own better ones. Like me, my dogs have had the advantage of a lot of experience to overcome any hereditary deficiencies. I'm sure that Jake, an English pointer who was my first really good pheasant dog, became so proficient at retrieving simply because I gave him so many cripples to chase.

In short, what distinguishes me from most of you is the extent of my experience and the fact that I've taken the time to record it. My goal is to share that experience with you. I think that you will be able to identify with much of it, and I hope that you will enjoy it. Although you may well learn from it as well, as I have from rereading my own hunting diaries, it is not my intention to try to teach you. I hunt pheasants for pleasure, and I wrote this book for my own pleasure and that of those pheasant hunters who read it.

This book deals strictly with hunting pheasants and with

other topics related directly to hunting, such as guns, loads, and dogs. Although the natural history of the pheasant is fascinating, game biologists can do a much better job with that subject than I could hope to. Likewise, a pheasant dinner can be a true culinary masterpiece. But for pheasant recipes, I'll refer you to any number of wild game cookbooks written by chefs of far greater talent than me.

Pheasants are legal game in most of the United States, the exceptions being the Southeast and the desert Southwest. I make no effort to summarize bird populations or hunting regulations in any of those states. Both have a way of changing, sometimes quite significantly, from season to season. Sporting magazines often publish pheasant forecasts in the fall, broken down by region or state. For even more specific and timely information, I suggest that you contact the game agency in the state where you are interested in hunting.

Likewise, most shooting preserves offer hunting for released pheasants. Although I will discuss preserve hunting in general, trying to list preserves in a book format would be even more futile than talking about state-by-state hunting opportunities. The preserve business is booming in many areas, and my information would be out-of-date by the time you read it.

When I first got the idea for this book, I had difficulty figuring out how to organize it. I knew that my diaries provided a wealth of material. But should I arrange it chronologically, starting in 1973 and ending with last season? Although that might make sense to me, it seemed that it would not be the best organization for you, the reader. If I'm talking about winter hunts, or opening day hunts, or dogs, or guns, why not group the information topically? This also gives you the option of skipping around. Although the chapters follow as logical an order as possible, they can be read individually and in virtually any sequence. If you want to read about dogs, then turn to "The *Real* Pheasant Hunters" first. I hope to eventually capture your interest to the extent that you will want to read the entire book.

Now that I've told you what the book is, what it isn't, and how it's organized, all that remains is for me to wish you good reading and good hunting.

From a Pheasant Hunter's Notebook

The Evolution of Pheasant Hunting

T is nearly noon on a mid-November day. Nine men are gathered around a couple of cars parked at the end of a cornfield. Guns cradled in the crooks of their arms, they smoke a last cigarette or gulp down the remainder of a thermos of coffee. A pair of teenagers in the group, a bit nervous and slightly apart from the others, check the shells in their pockets for the twentieth time. One breaks open his single-shot 20 gauge and peers down the bore, insuring that it is not obstructed.

A man of about 50, wearing a red plaid cap and carrying a 12 gauge pump with most of the bluing worn off, glances at his watch. "Almost noon, boys. Time to go. Ed, you take the left. Bill, you're on the right side. Boys," he says, addressing the two youngsters directly, "Remember what we've told you. Keep in line. No shots straight ahead once we're past the middle of the field. Uncle Joe and Tom and Charlie don't appreciate getting peppered with pellets." The other hunters laugh at this reference to the three blockers waiting at the far end of the field.

"When you've got a bird down, make sure you get there quick," he continues. "And let's try to shoot all roosters this year, boys," he adds for everyone's benefit. "They're the ones with the pretty feathers and long tails." Everyone laughs.

The group fans out across the eighty-odd rows of standing corn, waiting for the leader to give the signal. He glances at his watch again. "OK, let's go!" he yells.

The browns and tans of their hunting coats blend in with the yellow of the dried corn stalks and foxtail, broken only by the

3

occasional red splotch of a cap. The line moves forward at a steady pace down the quarter-mile-long rows, hunters spaced about ten rows apart. The object, as they all know, is to herd the pheasants in front of them. They hope the spacing is tight enough to prevent any birds from hunkering down as the line passes by.

The hunters exchange casual comments as they walk, as well as passing on an occasional warning to the two novices to stay even with the rest of the line. Some hundred yards into the field, one of the boys spots birds on the ground. "They're running ahead of us!" he yells.

"Just keep going," yells the leader in reply. "Go ahead and shoot one on the ground—if it's a rooster and if it's close enough. But watch your shots!"

At that moment, a rooster explodes two rows to the right and directly behind one of the youths. "Rooster!" he cries. A few seconds of silence. A gun booms off to the far right. "Bill got him," the word comes back down the line. There is a brief pause while Bill jogs out into the pasture to the right of the field, where he claims the first bird of the day.

"Ready down there?" yells the leader. "We're set again," comes the reply down the line. They move on. One of the youths nearly steps on a hen. His gun is up to his shoulder and the hammer back when the yell "Hen!" from the hunter to his right stops him short.

More shots sound along the line. Two roosters are bagged, and a third hits running. The bird is out of range on the ground, and the experienced hunter realizes the futility of chasing as the wing-busted cock sprints down the corn row.

"Cripple running ahead," he calls. "Maybe it'll squat down where we can get it at the end of the field."

The line has now reached the halfway point. "Watch your shots ahead now, boys," calls the leader. The experienced hunters check their safeties in anticipation. They know that the bulk of the action will take place within the next few minutes.

At the far end of the field, three men kneel in a ditch. Spaced about 35 yards apart, their job is to stop the birds from running out of the far end of the field. All three are experienced pheasant hunters, veterans of many drives such as this. They were selected as "blockers" based on this experience, their marksmanship, and, in the case of Uncle Joe, his excess weight and arthritic knees. All three carry 12 gauge repeaters—a Winchester

Model 12, a Remington, and Joe's pride and joy, a Browning auto-loader with its distinctive, humpbacked silhouette. There are other similarities among the firearms: all are choked full and have 30-inch barrels, and all serve double duty in the duck marshes.

Joe peeks up over the edge of the ditch. The blockers are fortunate enough to have a position which will keep them out of sight of the pheasants and out of the line of fire of the oncoming hunters. However, they are not overly concerned with the latter. Most other members of the party are family members, and all are experienced hunters—except the two youngsters, who have been well coached in safety procedures.

"Can't see 'em yet, but I hear 'em coming," says Joe in a loud stage whisper to the other two, as he slides back down.

They hear shots from the drivers in front of them. A rooster comes streaking over Tom's head, in the middle of the trio. He spins with surprising speed and drops the bird in an open field across the dirt road behind them. The bird hits hard, but gets up to run. Tom finishes him off on the ground.

"Little behind that one, Tom," chides Joe.

"Son of a gun was really moving," replies Tom with a grin. "A guy forgets how fast they can fly from one season to the next."

Two birds sail over Charlie's head, on the opposite end of the blocking corps from Joe. "Hen! Hen!," he calls twice.

"After last year, I thought you shot them regardless, Charlie," needles Tom.

"Aw, shut up," he replies. "The sun was in my eyes on that one, and I don't suppose you'll ever forget it."

At that moment, a huge rooster, 2-foot tailfeathers streaming behind him, explodes from a clump of weeds at the end of the field, almost on top of Joe. Tom and Charlie watch with fascination as the old man tracks the escaping rooster. His Browning booms, and the bird drops over 40 yards from the gun.

"You're slowing down, Joe," calls Tom.

"Just letting him get out so's I don't shoot him up too bad. Martha gives me a bad time about too many pellets in the birds," he explains.

By now, the line is within 50 yards of the fence which marks the end of the field. Birds are flushing in threes and fours. Multiple shots and cries of "Hen!" and "Rooster!" echo up and down the line.

Within 15 yards of the end of the field, a big rooster erupts directly in front of one of the youths. Gun up and hammer back in a flash, the youngster drops the towering bird in a cloud of feathers.

"Nice shot, boy!" cries Tom from the ditch below, as the youngster comes forward to claim his prize. "You nearly dropped that one in my lap!"

The youth beams. His first pheasant ever!

The men cross the fence and confer with the blockers on the far side. Tom crosses the road to pick up four birds dropped in the open field on the other side. They collect their bag from the field. Fifteen roosters met their demise from that single, half-hour operation.

They compare notes. At least three more birds were hit in the air but not dropped, and three or four others brought down but not recovered. The leader pronounces the operation a success.

"Birds must be down a bit, though," comments Joe. "That field's usually good for a couple dozen at least."

Three hunters—the two youngsters and one other—take the birds back to the cars. On the way, as they walk the edge of the field, a tight-sitting bird takes wing right beside them. The veteran drops his load of birds and adds a sixteenth victim to the total.

A second cornfield yields a dozen more birds. The end of the day comes exactly at 2:35 in 40 acres of hay, where the hunters have observed that a number of escaping birds have taken refuge. A rooster sits so tight that the as-yet birdless youth nearly steps on it. Appropriately enough, it makes bird number thirty-six, and the dozen hunters have limited out.

Scenes such as the one above were replayed across the Midwest with regularity until as recently as the mid-1960s. Pheasant hunting was mostly a group sport, and opening day in particular was a festive occasion. Using the block and drive method on cornfields was the preferred tactic for taking pheasants, especially early in the season.

That tactic worked well then for several reasons. Cornfields tended to be relatively small and could be covered by a group of a dozen or even fewer hunters. Corn was shorter and easier to shoot over than it is now. Finally, the use of herbicides was less common, leaving more weedy cover in the corn rows to provide hiding places for the birds.

That method was also logical because of the way game departments had set up shooting hours and seasons. In Iowa, for example, the season opened in mid-November and only lasted for about a month, until 1963 when it was extended through the end of the year. Shooting hours usually started at noon, or certainly no earlier than nine or ten o'clock. (That tradition still holds in South Dakota. The season opens there in mid- to late October, with shooting hours of noon to sunset. After November 1, shooting hours begin at 10:00 A.M.)

There was almost always a fair amount of corn left to be picked by the time the opener rolled around. The late start to shooting hours usually put the birds out feeding in the fields when hunting began. Hence the effectiveness of the cornfield drive on pheasants of a generation ago.

Gun selection was a direct result of the favored hunting tactics. Cornfield shots can be long, calling for a tight choke. Hunters with dogs found that the animals did not adapt well to running birds in standing corn, which meant that canine assistance was rare. To reduce cripple losses, hunters opted for the combination which they thought would produce the most certain kills. Twelve gauge full choke, the favorite in duck blinds, was also the choice of most midwestern pheasant hunters.

I remember those days well, although with less nostalgia than do many of my pheasant hunting contemporaries. They tend to forget the short seasons and abbreviated hours. And it's equally easy to forget all the crippled birds which went unrecovered in the corn.

But I must admit that at least part of my opinion about the "good old days" can be chalked up to sour grapes. Although I remember seeing those mass drive operations and hearing about them firsthand from my best friend—whose ten- to twelve-person family group always limited out on opening day—I seldom participated. I grew up the member of a group which was about as welcome by the big party hunters as the James Gang at an 1880s bank. My father brought me up in the tradition of the road hunter.

Dad was not only law-abiding, he was highly ethical in all his other hunting and fishing practices. We didn't exceed our limits while fishing, and we didn't hunt without permission. But there was something about pheasants which brought out my father's outlaw side.

I think it may have been the fact that he first shot pheasants during the Depression, when everyone looked the other way at bending game laws if it meant putting meat on the table. We also lived in what was then just about the best pheasant area of a very good pheasant state. It was hard to visualize the possibility of hurting the bird population.

Not that Dad would exceed his limit, as did some greedy hunters who would shoot three birds, drop them off with a farmer, and return to shoot three more. It was his method which was often illegal and almost always unethical.

The party hunters tended to drive surviving birds into odd spots of cover. The ditches and fencerows along secondary roads could be very productive for those who knew how to road hunt.

With us, it was a family affair. My older brother and I did a bit of it, but I remember it as being more effective when both Mother and Dad were involved.

Dad was the driver and principal shooter. Mother was the scout. I was the backup scout, and as I grew older, the backup shooter as well.

Road hunting was simplicity itself. Dad drove the back roads. Mother spotted pheasants in the ditches. Dad stopped and shot them, usually without bothering to get out of the car. If he had to get out, for example when the bird was on the opposite side of the car, he still shot the birds on the ground. Illegal in the first case, unethical in the second.

My parents were a great team. Mother could spot a rooster with his head half an inch out of the weeds from a car moving at 35 MPH. Dad always carried his .410 single-shot legally, unloaded and in its case. He was very adept at loading it in the close confines of the car and as safety-conscious as possible about not cocking the hammer until he had it out the window.

There may have been another reason for his tactic. He was a night shift factory worker who spent most of his adult life making John Deere tractors. He'd come home in the morning, catch a few hours' sleep, then drive out into the country for a quick hunt on the back roads near our home in Waterloo. There weren't that many other people who could have hunted during the week with Dad, and with a very physical job, he wasn't in need of exercise— just a change of scenery and a chance to put some meat on the table.

For whatever reason, I immediately sensed that this kind of hunting was wrong. It may have been that I read too many outdoor magazines with their discussion of the ethics of fair chase. Maybe I didn't like the ringing sound I'd have in my ears for half an hour after touching off the .410 from the car. Perhaps the thought of going to jail over a pheasant was sufficiently un-

pleasant. In any case, I was very uneasy over the whole procedure.

Although we were definitely breaking the law by shooting
from the car, we were not all that much less ethical than many of
the party hunters who looked down their noses at those of us who
shot most of our birds within 100 yards of the car. Dad, my
brother, and I all shot .410s, yet we probably crippled a smaller
percentage of birds than did the big bore-toting cornfield hunters.
We took our shots close and mostly at sitting birds. When we
were unsuccessful, it was usually because the bird ran or flew
before we were in position, not because we'd hit the bird and lost
him.

Also, there are some skills necessary to being a successful
road hunter. It's not all that easy to get within .410 range of a
sitting pheasant. When birds do flush, you have to get that little
gun on target quickly if you expect to make a kill. Growing up
with a single-shot .410 is undoubtedly why I still tend to rush
pheasants more than I need to.

My own version of road hunting was to get out and walk
likely looking ditches and railroads. After spotting enough
pheasants from the car, I got pretty good at figuring out which
ditches were the best bets to hold birds. These narrow strips of
cover were perfectly suited to a hunter or two working without a
dog. You could even work a two-person drive, which usually involved me walking and either Dad or my brother driving ahead a
few hundred yards, then getting out and blocking for me.

I also developed a couple of methods of working birds we did
spot in the ditches. From long experience, I learned that a
pheasant would nearly always run or fly if you stopped a car and
got out in close proximity. However, if you could make your approach from farther away with some sort of cover, you stood a
chance.

Using the opposite ditch is one tactic which worked very
well. If I spotted a bird, I'd try to remember its location in relation
to a landmark such as a telephone pole, tree, or fencepost. Then
I'd proceed down the road a hundred yards or so, stop the car,
and get into the opposite ditch. I'd stay below the crown of the
road, keeping my eyes peeled for the landmark. Once it was in
sight, I'd charge across the road, hoping to surprise the bird into
flushing. It worked fairly often.

If the opposite ditch wasn't deep enough to offer me cover, I'd
use the car itself. Once again, I'd pass the bird by and continue
for at least 100 yards. Then I'd have the driver turn the car

around. I'd walk on the opposite side of the car from the bird, and with the car moving very slowly and giving me cover, I'd work up to my landmark. Once there, I'd let the car continue on and charge the spot where I'd last seen the bird. Unlike stopped cars, moving cars seldom spook pheasants. This variation of the cover tactic worked well also.

I am giving all of the above only as historical background, both of pheasant hunting in general and of my own development as a pheasant hunter. I am well aware of the fact that road hunting, whether you're inside or outside of the car, is totally illegal in many states. Although I will still ditch-sneak a bird on occasion, it's mostly for nostalgia. It's certainly not the way I prefer to hunt, nor is it a good example to set for young hunters. It is simply too easy to cross over the line into unethical or illegal behavior. Finally, it is much less effective now than it was during my own learning years.

Road hunting worked well thirty years ago for many of the same reasons which favored the cornfield drive. In those days, Iowa pheasants were mostly concentrated in the northern half of the state, and some of those concentrations resulted in unbelievable numbers of birds in certain areas. The short season and hours also concentrated the hunting pressure, meaning that the birds were being pushed all over. Add to this the pheasant's need to pick gravel in order to digest its food, and you have a situation which is tailor-made for road hunters.

Times change. Some of those changes are for the better, some for the worse. The end of the Soil Bank in the mid-1960s was not one of the better changes, either for the birds or the hunters. Farming grew more intensive, and with less nesting and winter habitat, bird numbers fell.

That was pretty much the pattern from the mid-1960s to the mid-1980s. Pheasant populations shifted to those areas which afforded the birds the proper mix of food and cover. For the most part, these were areas where intensive row-crop farming was impractical. But even the best areas fell far short of the concentrations of birds which were relatively common before the end of the Soil Bank.

The 1985 farm bill is the most recent significant change in the world of the pheasant and the pheasant hunter. The program has already retired millions of acres of marginal farmland, much like the Soil Bank. This provision of the bill, the Conservation Reserve Program (CRP), has led to a dramatic upsurge in pheasant populations wherever the CRP has been widely accepted. Iowa pheasant hunters accounted for nearly a million and a half birds in 1987, a figure that leading pheasant state had not approached for a number of years.

The severe drought of 1988 was a step in the wrong direction, although optimists hope it was only temporary. The drought emergency resulted in widespread mowing of CRP acres to relieve a shortage of hay for livestock. A lot of valuable pheasant cover was destroyed. Time will tell how much long-term damage was done, but it appears likely that the CRP ground will be restored to permanent grasslands barring another similar dry year.

But not everything which happened between 1965 and 1985 has been bad for pheasant hunters. The dramatic drop in bird numbers resulted in a parallel decline in hunter numbers. Most of these were the once-a-year gang, the nimrods who went out for the easy pickings on opening day. With a resigned sigh and a complaint of "It ain't like it used to be," they returned to the couch and the Saturday football game to which they were better suited in the first place.

While equally unhappy with the decline in bird numbers, other hunters developed new tactics. Widely scattered birds meant that it was necessary to cover more ground in order to find game. Coupling this with the fact that a pheasant in the bag was now a highly prized commodity, more hunters took to using dogs, both to locate scattered birds and to cut down on cripple losses. In the Midwest, duck hunters were among the first to make this switch. They discovered that their Labs could be as valuable in the uplands as they were in the marshes.

Such changes did not occur overnight. Pheasant hunting never had developed a hard-core contingent of devotees like grouse, woodcock, or quail. It had always been an easy game, with its participants unused to the adversity grouse hunters experienced in a down cycle, woodcock gunners learned when they didn't catch the flights, or quail shooters knew would follow a harsh winter.

Outdoor writers were also at fault, at least to a certain degree. Outside of an occasional bit of grudging admiration, mainly as a result of the pheasant's appeal to the masses, where were the hymns of praise to the ringneck? The grouse had its Burton Spillers and William Harnden Fosters, the quail its Nash Buckinghams and Havilah Babcocks. The best press the pheasant received in those good old days was probably a photo of a pile of dead birds in the *Des Moines Register.* Like Rodney Dangerfield, the pheasant just didn't get much respect.

In my own case, it took the odd combination of a classic grouse writer and a Moroccan-born Brittany to show me that pheasant hunters needed to reevaluate their attitudes.

I left the Midwest in the late 1960s and returned in 1973. In between, I read George Bird Evans and shot chukar and European quail in Morocco with a side-by-side shotgun over my first hunting dog. When I returned to Iowa, I brought the dog and the gun with me, along with my new approach to hunting.

For a brief period of time, grouse and woodcock were my first love. Although I now find it hard to believe, my notebooks remind me that there were a couple of years when I actually fired more shells at woodcock than at pheasant—all without leaving the state of Iowa, which even in its worst years is much better ringneck country than it is woodcock territory.

Gradually, the truth began to dawn on me. Grouse and woodcock are extremely sporting birds, but mostly so because of where they are found. It's tough to shoot any bird you can't see, and dense forest cover often makes it difficult, if not impossible, to even shoulder your gun when the bird does make a fleeting appearance.

The pheasant has no such advantages. He lives in places where, in comparison to grouse and woodcock cover, shots are nearly always open. When he flushes close at hand, he is none too fast about getting into the air and relatively easy to hit.

But that isn't the end of the story, as any pheasant hunter knows. The pheasant survives, when he does, because he uses his legs rather than his wings. He runs like Carl Lewis and, like Muhammad Ali in his prime, just isn't there anymore when you're ready to take a crack at him.

Hitting a pheasant is only half the battle. A ringneck is just about the toughest bird most upland gunners will ever encounter. A couple of 8s will put down a grouse, woodcock, or quail, none of which is likely to run very far even if still very lively when it is brought down. You can't count a pheasant as a sure thing until he's safely tucked into your game pouch, and putting him there can be every bit as much of a challenge as knocking him out of the air in the first place. That kind of tenacity, in my book, is worthy of a healthy dose of respect.

Yet the pheasant continues to get short shrift when compared to those "classic" upland birds. Hard-core ringneck chasers who have never seen a grouse or woodcock think that hunting old ruff must be the nearest thing to heaven on earth. I've now done plenty of both, and I'm here to tell you that the pheasant should not be shortchanged.

One reason I wanted to write a pheasant book is to emphasize that very point. You can hunt pheasants over solid pointing dogs and shoot them with a classic double, like I do, just as you can grouse, woodcock, or quail. You can also chase them with a champion retriever and a smooth-as-silk pump, as do other pheasant hunters. The "classic" aspect of the sport is in your attitude toward the game, not in any inherent advantages or deficiencies on the part of the bird. I firmly believe that, with bird numbers and habitat as they now are in many parts of the country, pheasant hunting stacks up favorably with the best upland gunning to be had anywhere.

I doubt that I need to convince many readers of this book of the pheasant's quality as a game bird. If I did, you probably wouldn't be reading it in the first place.

A generation ago, however, the pheasant might not have been worthy of comparison to New England ruffed grouse or Dixie bobwhites. But we pheasant hunters often ignore the fact that it is more a combination of the bird *and* its habitat which make for great sport than just the bird itself. Rocky Mountain hunters tree-shoot ruffed grouse for camp meat, and they're often able to get close enough to take the trusting birds with .22 pistols. Grouse aren't hunted out there like they are back East or up around the Great Lakes. Even in the Upper Peninsula of Michigan, where I've hunted grouse, many birds are taken from vehicles on tote roads, much as Dad and I used to take pheasants years ago.

In the Midwest in particular—especially the prime pheasant states of South Dakota, Nebraska, Kansas, and Iowa—we're now seeing a combination of bird numbers and good cover, which result in a kind of pheasant hunting radically different from that of thirty years ago. Standing corn is usually hard to find once the season opens, and if the farmer will let you hunt it, the birds will still run just like they used to, or even worse because of the lack of weeds. The really productive hunting takes place in other spots, such as set-aside fields, draws, and waterways.

Because bird concentrations aren't what they used to be, and because additional dog power, as opposed to additional manpower, is what is required in most cases, smaller hunting parties are much more effective. I wouldn't know what to do with one of those old twelve-person pheasant hunting squads anymore, but a

A generation ago, pheasant hunting was almost exclusively a group sport. Although the birds are still occasionally hunted by large parties, smaller groups of no more than three or four hunters are likely to be more effective.

couple of good dogs can produce enough birds so that a group of three or four hunters should be able to bag a limit halfway through opening day—if their shooting is equal to the task.

My appreciation of modern pheasant hunting began when I started using Deke, my Moroccan Brittany, to help me hunt the birds. Deke adapted very quickly to woodcock and bobwhite, which are tight-sitting birds like those he knew in Morocco. Although he never became a first-class pheasant dog, his occasional points and uncanny retrieving ability made him a valuable companion. I began to prize points on roosters, and kills over point, much as George Evans did in his experiences with West Virginia grouse. I also learned that simply knowing from a dog's actions that there are birds in the vicinity can be a great help to a pheasant hunter. After Deke, I never wanted to be a dogless hunter again.

Deke often operated without a lot of support from his human companions. My shooting was far worse in his first season on pheasants than it is now. Although I was using a 12 gauge double then, I think my pheasant shooting instincts were still operating as if I were using that old break-open .410. I missed pointed birds which should have been easy. On one occasion, that old single .410 malfunctioned in my brother's hands when Deke had the rooster pinned. Had Deke been human, he probably would have sought out a more capable group of hunters.

Within the first week of the season, however, Deke made a couple of memorable retrieves. The first one came the second day of the season. Unused to a dog's abilities, we were already resigned to having lost a downed bird when Deke brought it to hand. It was the first time I had seen that kind of dog work on a cripple, and it seemed almost miraculous to me.

The next weekend, Mark Hanchar dropped two roosters as we worked stripped standing corn in a field where the farmer was finishing his combining. We got one, but with the combine coming through, we had to get out of the way before we could find the second. Birds are notoriously hard to mark in standing corn. Deke found that bird on the next pass through the field. In the three short seasons Deke and I hunted pheasants together, I came to expect retrieves like that, and he seldom let me down.

Deke was replaced by an Irish setter named Nick. I'm still convinced that somewhere in the depths of his skull that dog harbored some deep-seated hunting abilities. Bringing them to the surface was beyond my capacity as a dog trainer. I began to wonder if good pheasant dogs were as rare as writers used to say they were, back in the days when most pheasant hunting was done in the corn. A bad dog can ruin hunts, and Nick often found himself relegated to the back of the station wagon because I refused to let him ruin anyone else's.

An English pointer named Jake, with whom I initially had some control problems, was my next hunting companion. Through a good bit of effort and the use of an electronic collar, I managed to modify Jake's habits a bit without dampening his

Because hunting conditions have changed, today a lone hunter with a good dog can successfully pursue the birds.

hunting desire. Jake produced a lot of birds for me, was the classic English pointer "statue" when he locked on point, and was an atypically fine retriever for that breed.

Jake was my first really good pheasant dog. Over the five and a half seasons he hunted, he averaged better than a productive point an hour on pheasants. Although pointing dog owners often get good results on ringnecks, most will admit that the majority of their shots don't come over point. In Jake's case, close to 60 percent of his pheasant kills were pointed birds.

When he died unexpectedly in the winter of 1986, I was as shocked as I had been by Deke's death ten years earlier. You may get another dog, but it never takes the place of the one you've lost.

This time, however, the loss was not total. An English pointer bitch named Rebel, Jake's daughter, took over where her father left off. Two and a half years old at the time of Jake's death and showing less promise than I had hoped, she developed quickly once I began hunting her as much as I had her father.

Through Rebel, Jake is still with me. She shares the kennel with Heidi, a shorthair bitch I acquired because experience has shown me the wisdom of having more than one dog. When I nearly lost Rebel to a kidney infection early in the fall of 1987, the value of having Heidi on hand became apparent.

Filling in solo for her recovering kennel-mate on a Michigan grouse and woodcock hunt, Heidi got the work necessary to ready her for her first pheasant season. We learned to operate as a team, and by the time the pheasant opener rolled around, Heidi was carrying more than her share of the load.

As I approach middle age, I've come to appreciate a dog which operates at somewhat less than the breakneck pace of an English pointer. Heidi is also typical of her breed in that she is a good natural retriever, a key quality in a pheasant dog.

With Reb now back to full capacity and available to handle those situations where I need a dog which can cover a lot of ground, and Heidi on hand to deal with the smaller, denser pieces of cover where I want a slower, more thorough dog, I have what I consider to be the near-ideal team for pheasant hunting in the 1990s. The dogs might opt for an owner who shoots a bit better, but they get plenty of work and more than an occasional test of their skill at retrieving cripples.

As we approach the twenty-first century, pheasant hunting has evolved into a challenging game which more closely resembles grouse gunning or quail shooting than it did a generation ago. Although some pheasants still fall to dogless hunters, every serious pheasant hunter I know owns at least one good dog. They do their hunting mostly in pairs, certainly very rarely in groups of more than four. They treat every rooster in the bag as a trophy and pride themselves on making every possible effort to recover downed birds.

The typical pheasant gun among the hard-core modern hunting contingent is different from what their fathers carried as well. The majority of serious pheasant gunners of my acquaintance carry doubles, either side-by-side or superposed. Twenty-six-inch barrels, usually choked improved cylinder and modified, seem to be the choice of most. What these hunters want is a light, fast-handling gun which they can carry all day but which has the capacity to throw at least an ounce of shot out to 40 yards or so with lethal effect. The advance warning a dog gives of the presence of birds makes for closer shots, and of course the dog makes recovering cripples more likely. Nevertheless, most hunters I know would rather bring the bird down close, preferably dead, and not risk cripple losses.

I'm much more comfortable with the kind of ethic surrounding today's pheasant hunting than I was with the cornfield gang hunting or road scouring tactics of my youth. It is a tradition I'd like to pass on to my son and to the other pheasant hunters of his generation. While not all change is for the better, I feel that the pheasant hunting of today is a better sport than it was a generation ago and that the majority of today's pheasant hunters are true sportsmen.

Through the Season

THOSE hunters who think that pheasant season begins on opening day are the same hunters who are likely to come home early, frustrated, and well short of their limits. Pheasant season should start at least a couple of months before the official opener, if not longer. That's what I feel is the minimum amount of time needed to get yourself, your shooting, and your dog in shape, not to mention finding a place to hunt.

I'll discuss conditioning, shooting, and dog training elsewhere. I'll also go into more detail about how to find places to hunt. In this chapter, suffice it to say that, at least in most states where the pheasant is heavily hunted, you need to make arrangements well before opening day if you expect to secure a good place to hunt.

In pheasant country, happiness to the ringneck hunters is arriving at their chosen farms opening morning, knowing they'll be welcome, and that they'll have a reasonable chance of a good day in the field. That "good day" means not only a few decent shots at birds but also having enough ground set aside for their parties so that they're not running into other groups every fifteen minutes. Even though shotguns are essentially short-range weapons, I get an uneasy feeling when I top a rise and see a line of hunters 100 yards away and advancing in my direction.

If you have hunting rights to such a spot, count yourself lucky. A friend got me on to a dandy Iowa County farm in the middle of the 1979 season, and I was so impressed with the bird population and the cover that I made arrangements to hunt the

19

opener there the following year. That tradition lasted for seven years and resulted in relatively easy limits on five of those trips. The other two years, late harvests and birds taking to huge fields of standing corn made it hard on opening-day hunters everywhere in Iowa.

I only made a change when too many people found out about the place and the friendly landowner found it too difficult to say no. I saw that it was trying his patience and moved my opening-day activities to an area which received less pressure.

Opening-day birds are usually regarded as easy pickings. This can be true unless standing crops cause a problem, as mentioned earlier. But in order to be successful on opening day, the hunter has to remember that things have changed significantly since the days of that group hunt I described in the previous chapter.

The first piece of advice I'd offer is to keep your opening-day party small. If you're trying to get permission for the opener especially, but for any other time as well, landowners tend to be much more receptive to smaller groups. I've never opened the season with more than three other hunters, and many times it's been myself and only one other gunner. Unless you're hunting standing corn, you don't need that much manpower. There may be a lot of pheasants in a large set-aside field, but what you need to find them is four-legged rather than two-legged help. They may also be quite scattered, and even with dogs, it may take you some time to cover the ground. But with a small number of hunters, you don't need to find all that many birds to keep everyone interested.

The second thing to remember, if you're in heavily hunted country, is that you're probably stuck with the farm you start on. Later in the season, if you hunt out one place, you can always move to another. On opening day, however, chances are good that you will find other hunters wherever you go in good pheasant country. That's why many opening-day gunners hunt out their ground, then head for home, even if they're well short of their limit and still able to do more walking. Although this sounds like a disadvantage, you can actually make it work in your favor.

Nineteen eighty-one was my first season with Jake, who was to show me what hunting with a really good pheasant dog was like. It was my second season opener on that Iowa County hotspot, and the year before I'd taken the limit without a dog—and missed a lot more birds than I hit.

We started out as a four-man group, but two of them de-

Early-season birds often sit very tight.

parted, birdless, at about ten o'clock for a University of Iowa foot-ball game. That left me and the farmer's son, with three birds in the bag and everything on the place hunted.

We drove to a couple of places belonging to the landowner's relatives, but there were hunters everywhere. Not surprising, be-cause it was an excellent year for pheasants and we were only about 5 miles off Interstate 80. There were out-of-state license plates everywhere.

Then I had a brainstorm. It was nearing noon, both Todd and I were hungry, and I offered to take him to town for lunch. Over a sandwich and french fries, I suggested that we return to his place and start all over again. To tell the truth, I didn't have a lot of confidence in that idea, but I was far from ready to call it a day.

My notebook reminds me that we started our afternoon hunt about one o'clock, in the very same field where we'd started at eight that morning. It was an 80-acre field, about half in picked corn, the remainder in pasture with a large, weedy draw at the far east boundary.

Working north along the west fence, Jake made a beautiful point in the weedy fence line, giving me an easy shot. We worked clear to the north fence and around that edge with nothing to show for it. But coming back down the east fence, through the draw, Jake produced two more solid points on roosters. One flushed before Todd was in range. The other waited too long.

The final bird flushed without waiting around for Jake, and I dropped it to complete our two-person limit. We'd taken those three roosters in less than half an hour, far better results than in the morning when it had taken us a good two hours to bag a trio of cocks.

I theorized at the time that all the hunting pressure in the vicinity was pushing birds back and forth all day. The field we hunted that afternoon bordered neighboring farms on two sides, and there were hunting parties both places. They could have chased birds over to us, or they might have chased birds back that we had moved in their direction earlier.

Could the birds have been there all the time? Pheasants can be tough to pin down early in the morning if they haven't moved enough from their roosts to put out a lot of scent. But having seen Jake work both preserve and wild birds in situations where I had to retrace my steps over areas we'd already hunted, I tend to discount the possibility of his missing many birds.

The 1984 opener gave me another chance to test the theory. Mike Carroll and I started our efforts in that same 80-acre field, but by 9:30 all we had to show were one miss by Mike and one rooster in the bag for me. With other groups hunting most of the rest of the farm, we decided to take a breather.

At 11:30, we were back in that north field again. This time it took Jake and the two of us about an hour and a quarter to bag three more roosters. We also spent the better part of half an hour looking for another one Mike brought down, but even Jake's best efforts couldn't locate it.

Most of the time on opening day, I've either shot well enough or had enough land to hunt that I haven't had to retrace my own steps. However, those two experiences tell me that it will probably be worthwhile if there is enough pressure on surrounding property to chase birds back and forth. In most good pheasant areas, I think that will be the case.

In 1988 and 1989, Iowa didn't make the conversion to standard time until the last Sunday in October, and the pheasant season opened on the last Saturday. This meant that we were, in effect, hunting at seven rather than at eight o'clock. On both occasions, we were putting up birds that the dogs were not scenting. I attribute that to the time difference, which caused us to catch roosting birds that had yet to move around much. Although this is just about the extent of my experience with early pheasant hunting hours, I'd say that hunters in those states with an opening time of sunrise or half an hour before would be well advised to hunt the same cover again later in the day. There may well be birds that you missed on the first trip.

Obviously, pheasants do move, and you won't always find them the same places. In Iowa, where we've had an 8:00 A.M. opening time for a number of years, finding birds first thing in the morning can be a bit tricky. If it is relatively warm and the sun is out, the birds may well have already moved out of roosting cover to feed. Likewise, if the cover is very wet, either from dew or melting frost, the birds may have left to dry off. Pheasants don't care for wet feathers.

On a cloudy, raw day, the birds are much more likely to be in or near the same places where they roosted the previous night. Those places are usually easy to identify by the matted-down depressions the big birds leave in the cover, along with the piles of droppings. If you find such signs, usually in a draw or along a weedy stream course, but there are no birds, keep the place in mind for future hunts early or late in the day when the weather is more likely to keep the birds in the cover. But for the time being, you're better off moving to grain fields, where the birds are probably feeding.

To the uninitiated, picked corn looks to be a poor place to hunt pheasants. In fact, just the opposite is true. Pheasants are masters at scrunching down under cornstalks. But the best places to look for the birds are along fence lines bordering such fields, and in any small draws, creeks, or depressions that run through the fields.

My first hunt on that Iowa County farm was an excellent example of what can happen in picked corn. That was a B.J. (before Jake) hunt, and Nick the Red Rocket, an Irish setter with a great disposition but a severe mental deficiency, was my canine companion.

Nick was acting his usual out-of-control self, and after he flushed a few birds out of range, I relegated him to his purgatory in the back of the station wagon and got down to serious hunting.

The season was only a couple of weeks old, and I was scouting out the farm for a group of outdoor-writer friends who were coming down for a Thanksgiving hunt. I wanted to make sure it hadn't been shot out on opening day.

I'm sure that Mark Smith, my hunting partner that day, thought I had a better nose than most bird dogs by the time the hunt was over. We hunted picked corn almost exclusively.

"Careful not to walk too fast without a dog," I told Mark as we worked opposite sides of a narrow creek. "You'll walk right by the birds."

A rooster flushed behind him as I finished my sentence. He was too surprised to shoot. Five minutes later, another came up in front of me, and I dropped it cleanly.

We moved across the road to a picked field with a couple of nice draws, plus some smaller strips of foxtail and other mixed cover.

"These draws are great," I told Mark. "You want to be particularly ready when we get to the end." Sure enough, where draw ran out into the corn, a rooster waited too long. It took me a second barrel on that bird.

"Don't overlook any of these small strips of cover," I told Mark, working out a little patch of foxtail as we walked through the picked corn. "Roosters don't need a lot to hide in." I was prophetic again, nearly getting my face slapped as a tight-sitting ringneck climbed past my head. Bird number three in the bag.

I broke my gun, three roosters in my vest, and Mark and I headed back to the gravel road. "Watch for birds in that ditch," I told him, as he lifted a leg to clear the three-strand barbed wire fence. He turned to say something, but the cackling rooster that flushed not 10 feet from him cut him short.

I don't really have a nose for birds, and I've found since that dogs are much better at retrieving as well as finding pheasants. It just happened on that particular day that there was a bird in virtually every likely spot. In years when the population is good, that can be the case on the opener and at least for the first couple of weeks of the season.

As mentioned earlier, hunting the pheasant opener is almost always good in decent ringneck country unless you have to contend with an excess of standing crops. What happens over the following few weeks will depend on a number of factors: the bird population, hunting pressure, and changes in cover.

A good bird population will often mean excellent hunting beyond the opener, despite hunting pressure. A couple of instances from my 1988 notes illustrate this clearly.

Although we did very well on opening day, the first two hours of the second day of the season found four of us with a single bird (and that a cripple left from the previous day and run down by my shorthair, Heidi). My three companions had commitments for the rest of the day, leaving me alone with a strong urge for more action.

Stopping off to see a farmer friend of mine in Poweshiek County, I found a large party of hunters on his home place. However, he gave me permission to hunt another 200-acre tract he was farming, located several miles from there. He did caution me that he and his boys had already hunted there that morning and took several birds.

I knew the place well. It didn't have a lot of cover, and I assumed that it had been quite thoroughly combed that morning. But it was past midafternoon, and Rebel was getting impatient in the kennel.

The farm stretched a full mile from north to south, and I had hunted nearly from one side to the other without action, except a single quail in a very unlikely spot. Then Rebel began her point-and-move routine, which told me we had a running bird. Although it never did hold for the dog, I was close enough to drop the rooster on a decent left-to-right crossing shot. That bird and the one Heidi had collected that morning left me one short of a limit.

Working a draw with fairly thin cover up to the buildings at the far corner of the place, we put up a big rooster at the fringe of range. Reb had done a nice job of nailing him, but earlier experience with hunters and insufficient cover resulted in the long-distance flush. I missed a difficult double try.

Swinging down the fence that headed back to our starting point, Reb crossed over with a nose full of bird. I was watching her to my right when the young rooster cleared cover about 10 yards to my left. The only excuse I can give for taking both barrels on that easy shot is the element of surprise. I broke the old 16 and we made the long walk back, my hunting vest satisfyingly heavy with the weight of a pair of roosters.

On the way out, Reb finished her day with a beautiful point on a young ringneck, minus a tail, that chose to bury itself in a patch of cattails by a narrow creek. The excellent opportunity made me wish I had been a bird short. In spite of having been hunted just that morning, that farm still held at least the four cocks Reb and I had moved. Obviously, the bird numbers there were quite good.

Four days later, I was back knocking on the same farmer's door along with my friend Steve Grooms. Steve had opened the season in extreme southern Iowa and had run into a situation just the opposite of what we were experiencing less than one hundred miles north. That part of the state, which for years had been Iowa's top pheasant area, had taken a nosedive. The reasons are still in doubt, but it appears that the very hot, dry summer of 1988, which hit that area the worst of all, took a severe toll on the birds. Reproduction and/or chick survival must have been almost nil.

When Steve called to inquire about the conditions in my area, I told him that they had been incredibly good to that point. In addition to two limits over the weekend, I'd taken three more birds in forty-five minutes the day before. I told him that my Iowa State teaching schedule wouldn't allow for an all-day hunt but that I could meet him first thing the next morning for a couple of quick hours in the field.

The farmer advised us that he figured at least a couple of dozen birds had been taken off his 400 acres by that time and that it had been hunted more or less constantly since opening day. However, we were welcome to give it a try. On that particular morning, at least, we would be the first ones through the cover.

The key feature of that farm, which I've hunted numerous times, is an excellent creek which meanders over a mile from the north end of the farm to the south. About halfway, there is a fork which makes the cover look like a giant Y if viewed from above. With the wind coming out of the south, Steve and I started at the upper end of the right-hand fork of the Y-shaped cover, at the northeast corner of the farm. The plan was to follow that arm to its junction with the other arm, and then work on south to the base of the Y. If there was no other particularly promising cover, we would then reverse our course, come back up to the junction, and take the left or unhunted fork out to the north road.

This narrow cover is quite thick in places and is much better suited to Heidi's style of hunting than Rebel's. I turned my shorthair loose, and she headed for the creek bottom. Steve's English setter, Spook, stayed up on top along with the two of us, hunting the lighter, more open cover much as Rebel probably would have.

We had action not much over 100 yards from where we left the car. Heidi pointed, and a crippled rooster scurried up the bank and across in front of me. The bank was too steep for her to get out easily, and I had to take the bird on the ground or risk having it escape.

We were nearly to the junction with the other fork of the cover before anything else happened. Heidi started tiptoeing, and birds began to bust out of the cover like crazy. One went Steve's way, then one my way, then another his way. He got both of his. I dropped mine on a long shot, but it still had legs and made a dash back into the cover. We called the dogs in, and Spook found it dead down on the bottom.

Moving on, we flushed another bird that Steve hit, but it flew on and went unrecovered. One flushed directly in front of me, straight into the sun. I couldn't tell hen from rooster, but Steve could and dropped it for his third. My own last bird came shortly thereafter, long before we'd hunted to the end of the cover.

Those six birds in just over half an hour are the fastest two-man limit I've ever been part of. Combined with my quick limit of the day before, I had averaged less than fifteen minutes per bird for the two days. Both places I'd hunted had had pressure, but the hunting was still excellent. Opening weekend crowds seldom shoot out the cover, especially when there are good numbers of birds.

Other entries from my notebooks tell me the same thing. In 1983, I took a three-bird limit in under half an hour on the first Friday of the season. Jake and I were working a small public hunting area located right on a major highway, and it had undoubtedly received a lot of pressure the previous weekend.

Two years before that, in my first season with Jake, that same area had given me a brace of birds in well under an hour at about the same point in the season. I could have had number three, which flushed while I was reloading, if I hadn't used both barrels to get number two.

In summary, what I'm saying is that the best hunting is not automatically over after opening weekend. In Iowa, the pressure drops off after opening weekend, but most of the nonresidents stay for several days beyond that. The state's twelve-bird possession limit encourages them not to leave too quickly, and a high percentage of the out-of-staters who come for the opener are quite likely to be around for most of the next week as well.

This is certainly the period of the most consistent and intense hunting pressure of the entire season. Yet my notebooks show clearly that good hunting almost always holds up for at least two or three weeks after the opener. By then, the pressure has dropped off a lot, especially during the week. Nonresidents will continue to come in throughout the season, but not nearly in the numbers of the opening week.

Of course there is the cumulative effect of the pressure to consider. Although we think of pheasants as fairly smart birds, most of the roosters in any given season have never been hunted before. It may take them several close encounters to adapt to human predators.

Again, the overall population may be a factor as well. If the hunters get birds quickly and easily, the ringnecks that hang out in the more out-of-the-way spots may not see humans all that often. Therefore, when hunters do start reaching those less-accessible corners, the hunting may seem to be every bit as good as it was on the opener.

Pheasant hunters need to remember that population and pressure are elements which must be considered together. While a good population can sustain a fair amount of pressure and still provide decent hunting, lack of pressure won't mean easy pickings if the birds simply aren't there.

During the 1988 season, I was working on a magazine article about pay-to-hunt operations. My research took me to southwest Iowa, where an outfit called Pheasants Galore, located in the town of Corning, runs a bed-and-breakfast operation which houses hunting parties with landowners and gives them a place to hunt as well.

It was mid-December, and the hunting had started to get tough. They put me up on a farm which hadn't been hunted for a month and even earlier in the season had not seen a lot of pressure. The place had good cover and was located in a region which normally had very good numbers of birds.

I hunted hard for the better part of two days and never saw a rooster in range—and only a couple on wild flushes, for that matter. After returning home from that disappointing expedition, I confirmed with the DNR what I already suspected: that particular area simply had a far lower bird population than normal that year.

But there is another factor in addition to bird population and hunting pressure which must be considered. That is the changes which are taking place in the birds' habitat.

In most places, the pheasant is closely associated with agriculture. In Iowa, farms undergo a drastic change from the beginning of October to the end of November. Standing corn becomes picked corn, and in many cases picked corn becomes a bare, plowed field.

Even if most of the crops are harvested by opening day, there will still be significant changes in the cover over the next month.

Picked corn, as mentioned earlier, will often still provide excellent food and cover. A plowed field provides virtually none of either. And picked corn which has been worked over by cattle or hogs for some time also loses much of its value for pheasants. Even the weedy draws and creek banks will get trampled into next to uselessness if livestock are there long enough.

This change in habitat may force the birds to look elsewhere for heavier cover, or it may force them into cover which is more sparse than what they normally prefer. In the first instance, they simply leave those places where you may have found them earlier in the season. In the second, they are almost certain to be more nervous and tend to run or flush wild, because they sense their vulnerability.

The answer, then, is to change your hunting areas as the season progresses. Look for better and better cover, and remember at the same time that you are hunting fewer and fewer roosters. As cover continues to deteriorate, you may want to focus on areas with less pressure. In such spots, the changes in the cover are less likely to have a drastic effect on bird behavior. Another option is to focus more on public hunting areas late in the season. In this instance, you're making a conscious trade-off—cover for pressure. Public areas almost always have very good cover, but they often receive a lot of pressure, thus offsetting the value of the habitat to a certain degree.

I've found that the trade-off is often worth making. In the first place, public areas may not get as much pressure as you think. They certainly get hit hard early in most cases, because nonresidents are either uncomfortable or unsuccessful in trying to gain access to private ground. But residents, on the other hand, usually have an easier time getting permission to hunt private land because of local contacts. For this reason, and because they assume (sometimes incorrectly) that public areas are being pounded, the residents often shy away from state game areas.

The biggest exception to this are those public areas which lie fairly close to major urban areas. In-state hunters from big cities often have the same problems as nonresidents in obtaining permission to hunt private ground. They end up focusing on nearby public areas.

I often make the error of avoiding public areas myself when I can get access to private ground. Looking over my notes, I am quickly reminded that I would often be better off hunting the public areas. This is especially true in those years when the crops are all picked for the opener and the early hunting is very good on private land. Eventually, as available birds are harvested, the survivors respond to cumulative pressure, and as the amount of cover on private ground is reduced, things start to get tough. Throw in a bit of foul weather, increasing the birds' requirements for decent cover, and the odds start swinging in favor of the public areas.

Under such conditions, give me a relatively large public area in good pheasant country, not too close to any major city, and I will almost guarantee you that you will find birds.

In 1988, I had consistent, if not spectacular, luck on a 600-acre public hunting area which was normally a marsh but which in that very dry year was virtually wall-to-wall pheasant cover. My notes show that I made five trips to the marsh, hunted just under twelve hours, and bagged five birds. I lost two others which I knocked down, due to a combination of the extremely dense cover and the very dry conditions, which inhibited good dog work. I didn't hunt the place for the first two weeks of the season, but after that I hunted it periodically right up to the end. I moved at least one rooster in range on each visit. As I said, certainly not spectacular, but consistent. Late that same season, I made several trips to good farms, during which I didn't even see a rooster.

Having spent all this time reading about population, pressure, and cover, you are probably wondering when I am going to get around to weather. I have saved it for last because I consider it to be of less importance than the other three factors. I know that may seem like heresy, but I have my reasons.

The pheasant is an incredibly tough bird. Biologists from the Iowa DNR tell me that they have never documented a single case of a pheasant starving to death. Even in the harshest of Midwest winters, pheasants have the equipment and the energy to dig down through deep snow and find enough to eat. Look at a pheasant's beak and legs closely and you'll understand why; although a lot of quail may starve in a harsh Iowa winter, pheasants won't.

Severe winter storms will kill pheasants without doubt. If the birds fail to reach adequate cover, they will suffocate when howling winds blow snow into their beaks. If they turn tail to the same winds, the snow can blow up under their feathers, melt from their body heat, and then freeze, encasing them in a block of ice.

But fortunately, this kind of weather isn't all that common, even in the upper Midwest. Iowa had a severe killer storm just after Thanksgiving in 1985, and then went through three winters which were virtually without blizzards.

My feeling is that, for the greater part of most pheasant hunting seasons in most areas, it is not weather which causes birds to change their habits as much as it is response to hunting pressure and to man-made reduction in available cover.

I do believe that there are two weather factors which significantly increase the difficulty of successful pheasant hunting. The first is very strong winds. While a bit of a breeze is a help in moving scent around for the dogs, it can be more than a good thing when it reaches the 25–30 MPH range. Wind tends to make just about all game species spooky, and when you're bird hunting and relying on a dog's nose, it creates an obvious second problem as well.

About my only good advice here is to hunt sheltered areas, such as deep draws, stream courses, and the lee side of hills and ridges. Other than that, be prepared for less than spectacular work from your dog and for wild flushes from overly nervous birds.

It is always critical to work good cover into the wind, but especially so on windy days. Strong winds carry sound a long ways on the open prairie, and pheasants can hear well enough as it is.

The second negative weather factor is rain. Fortunately, unlike wind, heavy rains are relatively uncommon during pheasant season in most places. When they do come, I have one piece of advice: stay home. If you have limited time, such as on an out-of-state expedition, you may not feel able to sit out a storm. Otherwise, forget it.

Although you will often find pheasants in wet places, such as marshes, it will normally be their feet that they are willing to dampen. They will go to great lengths to avoid wet feathers. These include such very unpheasant-like activities as perching in evergreens.

I've actually seen a number of birds run out from under solid points when it's raining. In fact, the major problem of hunting in the rain—other than keeping dry and warm, because rain during pheasant season is always cold—is getting the birds to fly. On one occasion, when the bird had the effrontery to squeeze under a fence and go trotting across an open field while Jake stood there frustrated, I blasted the soaked critter. I don't know if it was a cripple or not, nor did I particularly care on that day.

In short, my experience is that hunting in the rain produces very few good opportunities but a significant amount of frustration and discomfort.

Heat can be a comfort problem for two-legged hunters as well as the four-legged variety, although its effect on the latter is more severe because it makes scenting harder. Fortunately, like heavy rains, extreme heat—of the 70-degree-plus variety—is not all that common during pheasant season in most of the bird's range.

Dry weather is another factor which mainly affects dog work. Nineteen eighty-eight was the driest season I can remember. Clouds of dust rose from the ground with every footfall one made in picked corn. I knocked down and lost four birds that year, the most I've ever had go unrecovered. On many occasions, with the wind in our favor, my normally reliable dogs would miss birds that should have been easy finds. Other hunters told me of similar experiences.

I did not notice, however, that the drought seemed to have much, if any, effect on bird behavior. The main adjustments a hunter has to make in the face of extremely dry conditions is to encourage the dog to work slower and more thoroughly and to help it as much as possible in recovering downed birds.

Snow is one weather factor virtually all pheasant hunters must face at some point every season, perhaps even for the majority of some seasons. I enjoy hunting in the snow when it first comes. If it stays around too long, gets too deep or too crusty, or is accompanied by extreme cold, it can get to be a real pain.

The first snow of the year seems to confuse pheasants. Considering that the season is often a month or so old by the time the white stuff blankets the ground, it is surprising that the birds often act as if they've done a memory dump of their experience with hunters up to that point.

In 1975 I was still a relative novice at pheasant hunting with dogs. My Brittany, Deke, was about the only pheasant dog I'd ever seen work, and even though it was his third season on ringnecks, he never really did learn how to handle them. He was quite good on woodcock and bobwhites, both of which stay put under a point. Pheasants, on the other hand, aren't always so polite.

On Thanksgiving Day that year, we were hosting relatives. They weren't due to arrive until midday, which permitted me and Deke to slip out for a quick morning hunt.

We'd gotten about 4 inches of fresh powder snow the night

*Late in the season, hunting can be very difficult or
very good. But all late-season birds are trophies.*

before, the kind that makes skiers and bird hunters happy. I
picked a good railroad right-of-way not far from town.

Two cocks came up together about ten minutes into the hunt.
I dropped the first but missed a good chance at a double on the
second. Looking around, I found not a single track on the ground.
The cover was knee deep weeds and quite heavy. I've since
learned that in such a situation, the birds will simply hunker
down with the snow on top of the cover like an extra blanket on
the bed. Eventually, they will come out to feed, but they hadn't
done so at this point.

On the second stretch of tracks we worked, Deke nosed one
out from its roosting place. The surprised bird flew into a nearby
oak and proceeded to scold Deke from a branch. I was partially

screened by brush and was so amazed at this behavior that I couldn't believe it. That probably kept me from crashing through the cover, which almost certainly would have pushed the bird in the opposite direction. Instead, as luck would have it, the rooster tired of its game and flushed back my way, giving me an easy shot.

By now, it was after nine o'clock, and the birds were starting to move around a bit. Number three flushed wild in front of Deke, but I dumped him in the powder with a nice shot from my modified barrel.

Running birds tended to give Deke fits, and he in turn could give me fits when he pushed them too hard and flushed them out of range. These tight-sitting snow birds, however, were a different story.

I've seen the same thing happen several times since then on the morning after the first significant snow of the year. If there is one day out of the entire season when I particularly want to be in the field, other than the opener, that is it.

Heavy snow that stays around a long time makes bird hunting real work. Plowing the drifts for a couple of hours will tell you for sure whether your legs and lungs are in shape.

The worst condition is when a thin crust forms. It's probably heavy enough to support the birds, and perhaps even your dog, but almost certainly not you. You make more noise than you would walking through 2 feet of cornflakes, and it's considerably harder work. You probably won't get close enough to the birds to shoot, and if you do, you'll probably be so out of breath and so surprised that you'll miss.

One thing a lot of snow does is concentrate the birds into a very few spots where there is decent cover. This bunching effect makes for great shooting, if you can successfully get within range. It's hard to fool that many pheasant eyes and ears, and every other winged and furred predator is going to be working the same area as well. It's easy to understand why the birds get a bit jumpy.

Back in 1985, when we had deep snow and cold weather almost from Thanksgiving to the end of the season, it was either hunt those few remaining spots or stay home. I, for one, can't stand that much inactivity unless conditions are completely unbearable.

I spotted a flock of about two dozen birds on a spot not far from my home where I fortunately had permission to hunt at any time without stopping to ask. The first time I saw the birds, I was driving down a gravel road. Crossing a bridge over a fairly substantial creek, I spotted them pecking around like a flock of barnyard chickens on a wide, snow-covered sandbar below the bank.

That particular creek had banks which dropped close to 20 feet from the fields on either side. That very depth was undoubtedly one of the attractions of the place, providing excellent refuge from the howling winds. Those banks also dictated my initial strategy.

I wasn't actually hunting that day, but I'm seldom without a gun and a few shells in the vehicle during pheasant season. When I spied the birds, I had enough good sense to drive on, rather than slowing or stopping, which probably would have spooked them. I continued down the road, pulling into a field road several hundred yards from the bridge.

My plan was simple. With the birds directly below the high bank on my side of the creek, I could approach them unseen. The fluffy snow would muffle my movements.

It worked like a charm. Five minutes later, I was standing on top of the bank, above twenty-odd unsuspecting pheasants. About that time, one of them spotted me, and they all flushed nearly in unison. I must have been more surprised that the simple maneuver worked than they were, because I didn't pull a feather with either barrel! Those birds learned their lesson quickly, and I never caught them in that position again for the remainder of the season.

I did, however, discover that they were almost always somewhere along a half mile or so of that creek. The problem was getting at them. Their favorite spot was a little willow-choked peninsula which jutted out into the creek at one of the stream's few wide spots. That bit of knowledge, as it turned out, was of little use to me.

The problem was that none of my options for approaching their favorite hiding place worked very well. I didn't have the favorable angle that I'd used when I caught them under the bridge, and whether I walked the bank on their side or the opposite side, they'd always see me coming.

I tried coming at the spot from out in the middle of an adjacent field, at a 90-degree angle. That might have worked except for an overeager dog. Actually, it did result in one late flushing rooster in the bag, which was encouraging.

The last day I tried the creek bunch, as I'd taken to calling them, I decided to walk the ice on the stream itself. This was both quieter and easier walking than bulldozing my way through the deep snow.

As I rounded the bend which was within gunshot of the willow pocket, my anticipation increased. My thumb settled firmly on the safety, my trigger finger lying ready alongside the cold steel loop of the trigger guard. Fifteen yards . . . 10 . . . 5 . . . 1 foot in the willows—nothing. Nobody home. The quarter-mile walk back to the bridge was a disappointing one.

Just as I was about to scramble up the bank, I noticed another smaller willow pocket, not 30 yards away, on the other side of the bridge. When it's the last hunt of the season, you don't leave any stones unturned.

Even though this willow patch was quite near where I'd first seen the birds a couple of weeks earlier, I was skeptical. I had parked almost in sight of it. I walked at it straight across the ice, throwing caution to the winter wind.

I'd just planted my feet on terra firma when pheasants began erupting out of the willows, going all directions. One big rooster climbed nearly straight up, and I dropped him hard on the ice. I swung on a second, which had cleared the bank and had the north wind in his tailfeathers. It would have been nice to end the year with a double, but my lead must have been at least a bird-length short.

You don't get a lot of opportunities when winter has had its grip on the land for several weeks. When you do, they often come all at once. In other words, it's a long walk between birds, so don't mess up.

I've read that very bad weather, in the sense of extreme cold and a lot of snow, can make for super hunting. Outside of the birds' initial reaction to snow, which I described earlier, I have not found that to be true. For reasons I've just cited, I definitely do not care for bad weather over a long period of time.

Pheasants can be hunted in very severe weather with some success. Steve Grooms and a fellow Minnesotan arrived in Iowa to hunt pheasants with me on the heels of that 1985 Thanksgiving weekend storm. We went out in −50 windchill weather, and we did kill birds. It was neither easy nor comfortable, even with lots of clothing, and I tend to think the smart ones were my two pointers, Jake and Rebel, who refused to get out of their doghouses. Steve's springer hunted, and his friend's Lab positively frolicked in the snow! I enjoyed it a lot more when, after the storm broke, I was able to take off my ski mask, and when I didn't have to wait for fifteen minutes to get the numbness out of my fingers, even with heavy gloves on.

Yes, you can take pheasants under just about any weather conditions, and you are certainly likely to experience a wide variety during the course of the season. But there are times, perhaps coming with the wisdom of middle age, when I'd just as soon not pay the price.

Shooting Pheasants I

HE pheasant hunting fraternity is in a perpetual state of debate over two crucial questions: which breed of dog is best for ringnecks and what gun should a pheasant hunter use. If you are looking for a definitive answer to either of those questions, I suggest you search elsewhere. It's not that I'm at all hesitant about giving my opinion. I simply feel that there are too many variables in pheasant hunting to give any one "right" answer to those two dilemmas.

I'll get around to pheasant dogs later on. In this chapter, I'm going to give you my thoughts on pheasant guns and on the art of shooting pheasants. I'll continue that discussion in the following chapter by taking a hard look at the relationship of gauge, choke, and load.

There is so much discussion about the choice of a pheasant gun because so many different gauges and actions are employed by pheasant hunters. I've taken roosters with a .410, a 12 gauge, and everything in between. I'm sure that the 10 gauge sees occasional action on pheasants, also.

There are very good reasons why you see a little bit of everything being used on pheasants. For one thing, the other two upland birds which draw a strong following, the ruffed grouse and the bobwhite quail, have always been hunted more for sport than for meat. You have the mystique of the grouse, the "king of the game birds," his elusiveness and his explosive flush. With quail, you have the traditions of the Old South, with pointers locked up on a sundown covey.

Persons who hunted those birds, either inspiring or inspired by writers who praised them, were doing it for the experience itself. Pheasant hunting, on the other hand, grew up with a "let's put some meat on the table" sort of attitude. And that's pretty logical when you look at how many people you can feed with one rooster, as opposed to a grouse or a couple of quail.

So what you have with pheasants is much more of a popular sport—popular in the sense of being available to almost anyone. You didn't need a high-class setter or pointer, or a fine gun. If you wanted, you could hunt pheasants simply by driving the farm roads. (The same is pretty much true of grouse, but no one ever mentions that in print.)

The fact that lots of people hunted pheasants, toting whatever they happened to own in the way of a shotgun and probably without the assistance of a dog, is why pheasant hunting and pheasant hunters were largely ignored by "real" bird hunters, and by outdoor writers for that matter, for so long.

As recently as twenty-five years ago, or even less, pheasant hunting was still done the way I described in the opening chapter—gangs of hunters working standing corn, dogless for the most part. Guns of choice were probably the Winchester Model 12 or the Browning Auto, both in 12 gauge, and both sporting 30-inch, full-choked barrels.

But a lot of hunters bagged a lot of roosters with whatever happened to be available. My dad used a break-open .410 single shot, minus a front sight, with the forearm taped to the barrel. Of course, he shot a lot of them on the sit, but that wasn't all that unusual either. I started with the same type of weapon, plus a front sight, minus the tape, and with a barrel that wasn't yet threatening to wear through.

Of course, I wouldn't recommend that gun to a pheasant hunter, and perhaps that is a good place to begin this discussion. What should we eliminate when we talk about pheasant guns?

I'd immediately throw out two types of action and one gauge, and put two other gauges into the questionable category.

The actions I write off for the serious pheasant hunter are the single-shot and the bolt-action. Both have two distinct advantages: they are cheap, and they are light. That's where the pluses end.

You need two quick shots with a pheasant. You may hit a rooster in the air and fail to bring him down, in which case you should have another chance to hit him again. Or you may hit him and bring him down running. In that case, especially if you don't have a dog, you should also be prepared to hit him again. Neither the single nor the bolt-action gives you that chance.

Many parents start their children with a single, both because it's cheap and because, in the case of a hammer-type gun, you can tell immediately if the gun is safe. The problem is that your average youngster has one heck of a time getting the hammer back on most of those guns, especially when wearing gloves. Were I to choose a youngster's first gun based on cost alone, I'd go with a bolt-action and take the risk of trusting the young hunter to keep it in the safe position until ready to fire. Even better, a youth model, or used, pump-action is not much more expensive and gives a quick second shot when the hunter becomes sufficiently experienced to get one off.

The pump and the bolt-action both have another important feature for young shooters: the action has to be operated before a second shell is chambered. If you give a youngster an auto or a double, there is a good chance that he or she may forget to put the gun back on safe after cranking off a round. Although that situation can be overcome by allowing the novice to load only one shell, the higher cost of most doubles and autoloaders also makes them less practical for a beginner's first gun.

The one gauge I eliminate is the .410. I know that plenty of ringnecks have fallen to the little gauge, including quite a few that I've done in myself. In my case however, most of them were on the sit. Yes, you can take pheasants with a .410—but you're also going to have to pass up some very tempting shots, or risk crippling birds, unless you are a very skilled scattergunner. Unfortunately, many parents place .410s in their children's hands because they don't kick much. I'll risk a bit more kick for a gun that is much more likely to make clean kills.

The two gauges that I consider questionable are the 28 and the 10. The 10 will undoubtedly kill pheasants, but it's so much gun to carry that I can't imagine why anyone would want to if they had a choice. The 28 is a sweetheart to handle, and it will drop roosters at moderate ranges. A 28 is certainly a better choice for a beginner or for someone who is especially recoil-shy than is a .410. However, I cast a doubting eye on the stopping power of the 28 at the ranges I'd like to be able to reach. Note that I make that statement without having patterned the new 1-ounce 28 gauge loads, which might cause me to change my mind.

That leaves us with three gauges—12, 16, and 20—and three actions—pump, autoloader, and double. As far as I am concerned, any combination of those gauges and actions will give you the makings of an adequate pheasant gun.

I am sure that the pump would win a nationwide popularity contest among ringneck gunners. Pumps are relatively cheap and quite reliable. If there were a true traditional pheasant gun, the pump would be it. More on that later.

The autoloader holds down second place. Although generally a bit more expensive and a bit less reliable mechanically than the pump, the autoloader has two definite advantages: reduced recoil and a very quick second (and, if required, third) shot without manually operating the action.

Even counting both over-and-unders and side-by-sides, I have no doubt but that the double gun ranks last in popularity among the three recommended actions. Price is the main culprit here. A decent new double will cost you at least twice as much as a very good pump and a good bit more than most autoloaders as well.

The aftermath of World War II also saw a definite trend away from doubles. Returning GIs were used to the semiautomatic M1 rifle and carbine. They were enchanted with guns which gave them firepower—perfectly understandable, especially if that firepower has saved your life more than a time or two. Neither the M1 rifle nor the carbine has much to offer in the way of handling characteristics—the rifle in particular feels heavy and clumsy. But the result was that a pump or auto shotgun didn't have to feel particularly good as long as it worked well.

Another problem with doubles was that good American ones, like the Parker, L.C. Smith, Ithaca, and Fox, had virtually disappeared by the end of the war. They had become too expensive to produce compared with pumps and autoloaders, and without a solid market for them, their fate was sealed.

The European gun industry was also a casualty of the war. Although good European guns eventually found their way into the American market, that was long after the end of the war and the establishment of a strong preference for the single-barreled guns. When Japanese goods started arriving in the States, they were initially cheap, mass-produced alternatives to American brand names. Japanese shotguns did not really establish themselves here until long after their cars and their electronics had earned a reputation for quality.

Now the double is making a comeback. Although price will keep it from ever winning the pheasant gunners' popularity contest, I'd have to give the double my personal vote as the best choice for a pheasant gun.

The fact that I shoot doubles myself, and the fact that I have killed the vast majority of the birds I have shot since 1974 with a Sauer 16 gauge side-by-side, may make me a bit prejudiced on this issue. But I have more objective evidence to go on here than my own feelings. Just about every hard-core pheasant hunter I know shoots a double. In fact, if you see a pheasant hunter with a good quality double, you're safe to make one of two assumptions: either this person's got more money to throw around than he or she knows what to do with, or you've met a very serious pheasant hunter who has spent the extra bucks on the gun that he or she feels will do the best job.

Although I've come out as a clear supporter of doubles, let me back up a bit. Pumps and autoloaders have no real disadvantage as pheasant guns. They will kill pheasants every bit as well. In fact, most double shooters will tell you that they made their choice based as much on a somewhat elusive quality called "feel" as they do on performance.

A gun's feel is a bit hard to define. Most good doubles are lighter than a pump or auto of the same gauge and barrel length, but weight is not the whole story. How the weight is distributed is very important. With good doubles, that distribution tends to be very much between the shooter's hands. This at least gives the shooter the illusion that the gun is easier to carry and faster to bring into action. As much of that may be in the shooter's head as in his hands, but in shooting a shotgun, you need to believe in your weapon. A shotgun has to be more a part of the shooter than a rifle, because it is pointed more or less instinctively, not aimed. That is why so many experienced hunters are eventually drawn to the double and its remarkable "feel."

Most hunters spend several years shooting pumps or autos before they end up with a double. I never had that experience. Probably as a result of too much brainwashing by outdoor writers in my impressionable youth, when it came time to lay aside my little .410, I was convinced that a double was the gun for me.

Although I was drawn to side-by-sides, fiscal reality prevailed. Dad found me a good used Savage over-and-under 20 gauge with double triggers. It set me back sixty-five dollars, which included a pretty nice case. I wish I still had that gun.

I shot the Savage reasonably well, probably making more kills with the second barrel than the first. That may have been due to a tendency to rush the first shot, left over from my .410

days, or to the fact that I'm cross-dominant. By the time I touched off the second tube, I had closed my dominant left eye and was using the proper rear sight for a right-handed shooter. Nowadays that's all automatic.

The Savage was replaced very briefly, and not very effectively, by a 12 gauge pump. Although I've owned a couple of other pumps, I think that one was the only pump I ever used on upland birds. I was in Morocco at the time, where the only pheasants belonged to the king. I tried killing chukar with the pump, with little success. To my recollection, I have never even shot at a pheasant with either a pump or an auto.

When I parted with the pump, I knew that I wanted another double. The only question was whether it would be another over-and-under, or a side-by-side. My first choice was one of the light little Beretta 20s, but fate kept that gun out of my hands. Had I wanted a gun choked modified-full, I might be shooting that Beretta today. That was how the gun I examined at the Air Force rod and gun club in Spain was choked. But I insisted on an improved cylinder-modified combination and put in an order.

The Beretta came just before hunting season—with a badly cracked forearm. With chukar and quail to be hunted, patience was not the answer. The other choices in the rod and gun club inventory were the Winchester 101, then selling at a military price of under two hundred dollars (oh, for the good old days!), and an SKB 150 side-by-side. The club manager advised me that the SKB, a 12 with my preference of chokes, would be a better field gun than the 20 gauge 101, choked modified and full. I believed him and bought the SKB.

I soon found that the side-by-side was the gun for me. I'd never shot one before in my life. Between quite a bit of skeet shooting and lots of Moroccan quail, I became a halfway decent shot. In 1973 the SKB came back to Iowa with me, where it proved a potent choice for ringneck hunting.

My firearms inventory at that time also included a scoped 6MM Remington, which I'd initially bought for shooting wild boar in Morocco. As it turned out, rifles were illegal over there. You hunted boar with slugs—perhaps a better choice at close range than the 6MM, in any case. But with virtually nothing to shoot in Iowa with a 6MM, that gun became very expendable. In the summer of 1974, I found a 16 gauge Sauer in a gun shop in Waterloo. I'd just finished work on my M.A., and I figured the few bucks I kicked in on top of the 6MM were easily justified as my graduation present.

My Sauer is a very European-looking gun. It came with sling swivels attached, a semi-pistol grip, a cheek piece, and about the smallest splinter forearm imaginable. It was fairly obvious to me that the gun had been liberated by some GI during the war. I've never been able to uncover any background information on my Sauer. A letter to Sauer confirmed that my 16 was a prewar gun. Sauer, now located in West Germany, operated in what is now East Germany before the war, and as a result has very few records. I have to content myself with knowing that I have a German shotgun that is older than I am.

The Sauer carries so nicely that I'd scarcely mind even if I shot it poorly. The truth is, though, that for about fifteen seasons, I shot it better than any other gun I've ever owned. Then, in 1989, I went full circle and purchased an SKB 200E 20 gauge side-by-side. Its design is much like that original Model 150 I used in Morocco, except it has a straight English stock. It also has choke tubes, which are a bit rare on side-by-sides.

I discovered that I shoot that little 20 extremely well, perhaps even better than the Sauer, as difficult as that is for me to believe. In any case, both guns saw a fair amount of use on pheasants that year, and probably will from now on. It is probably apparent by now that I'm a real lover of good doubles. Although I'm sure that I'll never shoot one of the legendary London best guns, the current price of which is about the same as a new luxury car, I have owned a wide variety of nice side-by-sides. Among this group are several SKBs between the 150 and the 200E, a Browning, an L. C. Smith, an Ithaca, and a Hatfield. I've also had the opportunity to put quite a few shells through a Winchester 23 and a Spanish-made Grulla 2. But none shoot as well for me as the Sauer and my current SKB.

I'm sure that some readers of this book have a strong attachment to a pump or an autoloader, if not a Winchester Model 12 or a Browning Auto, then perhaps a newer Remington 870 or 1100. I would imagine that various specimens of those models have accounted for hundreds of pheasants over the years for more than a few ringneck deadeyes. If you fall into that category, don't change just because I happen to have a soft spot for doubles.

Between the over-and-under and the side-by-side, the choice is pretty much one of personal preference. Although I find over-and-unders and side-by-sides equally appealing in appearance and handling qualities, I simply do not shoot superposeds very well. But if you look at the guns used by champion clay bird artists, you'll be hard pressed to find any side-by-sides at all. The target smokers believe that the OU's single sighting plane is a definite advantage.

The wide profile of the side-by-side, on the other hand, can be an advantage in the field, where a bit less precision is required. The side by side also is a bit easier to load, because it opens with a shallower break. That, however, is more of an advantage in a duck blind than in the uplands.

Although the side-by-side has made a recent comeback, there are still more over-and-unders available. Neither has much of an edge in the cost department, although on the used gun market, SKB side-by-sides and Browning's BSS are both good buys compared with what you'll have to shell out for a new double.

But whether you allow yourself to be enchanted by a double or a fine pump or auto, you should definitely consider the gun's carrying and handling characteristics. You're likely to do a bit more walking between birds than they did back in the pheasant's heyday, and it will probably be in tougher cover.

Grouse and woodcock hunters certainly focus on the issue of how quickly you can bring a gun into action. So do quail hunters, who in some places around the country don't walk much farther than from the jeep to a brace of pointers.

Although a pheasant won't catapult itself into the air with the jet-assisted boost of a departing grouse, nor is it likely to dart behind trees like a woodcock, nor come up in bobwhite covey fashion like a swarm of bumblebees, a ringneck hunter does not have all the time in the world. Also, pheasants are more often hunted in nastier weather than their more famous feathered kin, meaning that the hunter is likely to be more encumbered by several layers of clothing.

The light, short gun, therefore, be it double, pump, or auto, has something to offer to the pheasant hunter as well. I wouldn't advise anything shorter than about 25 inches on a double, which equates with around 22 inches on a pump or auto, because a shorter barrel than that encourages poking rather than swinging. However, a longer barrel is only an advantage to those who feel they need it. Any edge gained by the shooter with a 30-inch tube—say, on long shots—is primarily in that person's head. That much barrel is not needed for accurate pointing, and it will certainly slow you down in comparison with a shorter gun.

Whatever your choice in pheasant weaponry, gun fit is critical. The gun has to point where you look if you expect to shoot well with it.

The simplest way to determine if a gun fits is to focus on an object (for obvious reasons, I like a picture of a flushing pheasant) with the gun at port arms. Then mount the gun normally, closing both eyes as you do so. When you open your eyes, if the gun is on target, it's a reasonably good fit. If you're buying a new gun, or if you're having trouble with an old one, try this exercise several times.

I'm one of those fortunate people who fall into that more or less "average" size range for which factory guns are designed. I find that most guns fit me pretty well right off the shelf unless the stock is odd or has been tampered with.

You may find that you need to change the length of your stock, depending on the amount of clothing you wear. If the stock is a bit short when you're wearing just a vest or light hunting coat, you can always use a slip-on pad. When you add a couple of extra layers at the tail end of the season, the gun may fit just right without the pad.

My own preference for a short, light gun is a relative thing. My Sauer has 28-inch barrels, but you have to remember that is equivalent to a pump or auto with a 25-inch barrel, which is shorter than most seen in the field.

I'm not a large person. I stand 5'9" and weigh 160–65 when I've been watching what I eat. I've been blessed with a pair of legs that have finished a few marathons and a bunch of 5-mile-plus races into my forties. More to the point for a pheasant hunter, they'll carry me through a lot of full days in the field. But my upper body isn't exactly the envy of Sly Stallone, and a very heavy gun can make me arm-weary long before my legs have given up. I want to be as ready to put that gun into action during the last hour of the day as I was when I first loaded up in the morning.

But you may ask whether it is possible to overdo the light, fast-handling thing. That can be a problem. More than a few roosters escape with their skins because hunters rush things.

The difficulty with pheasants is their unpredictability. They may come up in your face, lumbering like an overloaded helicopter, or they may boil up at, or beyond, effective range.

I've missed my share of the close ones. Several years ago, Tom Huggler and I were doing some mixed bag pheasant and quail shooting on a farm in southern Iowa. Rebel, at 1½, was just coming into her own. When she locked up in some heavy grass near the edge of a picked corn field, the cover told me it was

A hit like this means the bird will stay where it falls. Too often, poor shooting results in missed or crippled birds.

much more likely to be a pheasant than a covey. I crossed my fingers for a legal rooster and walked in.

Tom was off to my right, ready to back me up, when the cock came cackling out of the cover, streaming two feet of tail behind him. We both fired twice, and I'm quite sure that rooster was still in relatively easy range when the salvo ended. I'm also quite sure we didn't ruffle a feather. I don't remember what Tom's excuse was, perhaps surprise that I didn't kill the bird—although he's seen me shoot enough to know that there are few sure things. My own problem was that I was trying too hard to make a quick, clean kill over my young dog.

The really good pheasant shots don't miss chances like that. I try not to blow too many of them, because there are enough difficult opportunities where I really feel fortunate to connect.

Although pheasants have a reputation of being easy to hit, I think that it exists mainly among grouse and quail gunners. If you only hunt opening day birds, it's possible to get that kind of idea. In fact, from 1981 to 1988, I only missed one opening day rooster, and limited out six of the eight years. In 1985 and 1986, the only years I didn't bag a first-day limit, late harvests kept almost everyone in Iowa from having good openers.

The opening day bird I did miss, back in 1987, is one Mike Carroll will never let me forget. Right at the start of shooting hours, we'd maneuvered ourselves into position on either side of a small patch of horseweed at one end of an excellent fencerow. Promptly at 8:00, I sent Heidi into the cover.

I doubt if it was 8:01 when a big rooster came sailing out, giving me a perfect crossing shot. I was behind with the first barrel and didn't catch up with the second. Mike claims the reason he missed the bird that came his way was he was so astounded that I'd missed mine. It's convenient how my hunting partners use me as an excuse for their misses.

The myth of the pheasant hunter who doesn't miss is just that. I've hunted with some of the best around, and they all miss, unless they pass up perfectly legitimate chances. Back in 1979, I invited three writer friends who are also hard-core bird hunters— Steve Grooms, Tom Huggler, and Gene Kroupa—to hunt Iowa pheasants with me. Neil Montz, an old college friend, was serving as our guide in northern Keokuk County. (Neil is now a Methodist minister, and looking back on it, divine help may well have been involved on that hunt.)

We started the second day of our hunt in an evergreen grove beside Neil's brother's farm. It was about three weeks into the season, and Neil assured us that a wily rooster or two nearly always figured out by that time of year that the proximity of the farm meant safety. Neil was right. As our line advanced through the grove, a rooster shot out on Steve's end. It's rare when his Ithaca SKB superposed goes off and nothing falls. This time there were two reports with nothing to show.

That inauspicious beginning did not indicate what was in store for us for the rest of the day. That rooster from the grove was the first of fourteen we shot at, and it was the only one to make good its escape.

Just how well should a pheasant hunter expect to do? I've seen the figure of 40 percent offered up as a good average, and I'll agree with that if you are talking about birds bagged for shells fired. If you mean birds bagged out of birds shot at, I think a respectable pheasant hunter should go at least one for two.

In my notebooks, I've always kept track of kills per shells fired, although with pheasants, I think a strong case can be made for birds bagged out of those shot at as being a more appropriate approach. You can hit a pheasant well with your first shot and still need a second, or perhaps even a third, to bring down an especially tenacious rooster.

If I kill the first rooster I flush with my first barrel, miss the second one twice, and take bird number three with two shots, that gives me two birds for five shells, or 40 percent. That jumps up to two birds out of three shot at, or 67 percent. Few pheasant hunters keep track anyhow, although I think they might find the numbers of interest if they did.

My best season by far, not at all typical of my shooting average over the last ten years, was 1983. Due to job commitments and inclement weather at the end of the season, I didn't hunt as much that year as I often do. I bagged twenty-three roosters with thirty-three shells, which is just about 70 percent. I don't even like to think about my score based on birds shot at—it was twenty-three out of twenty-six. In fact, I hit two of the three birds that I didn't bag. One dropped and was lost, and my partner finished the job on the other. I had only one clean miss all year. I've had days which were considerably worse than that.

My friend Dave Prine says that keeping score is for the trap range. That might sound like an alibi, but those who have seen Prine shoot know that he doesn't need one. Maybe I do it on pheasants because George Bird Evans did it on grouse and woodcock. I think that it makes an interesting basis of comparison from season to season.

If you do keep score, and if you aren't bagging 50 percent of the birds you shoot at, there is room for improvement. Of the clay bird games, skeet is more readily available than sporting clays and offers all the angles you're likely to encounter on pheasants. Although it's a game that you can "groove" if you call for the bird with the gun at the shoulder, yelling "pull" with your gun down is much better field shooting practice. Allowing the puller to delay up to five seconds or so makes it even better. If you really get cocky, let the puller select high or low house at random.

One thing skeet will teach you is the importance of lead. This is critical in pheasant hunting, because crossing birds present a lot of target if you include the tail. Unfortunately for pheasant hunters, a lot of roosters finish the season minus tails but otherwise in perfectly good condition.

For most hunters, crossing birds are tougher to hit because

of the lead factor. When you do hit them, however, they are much easier to kill. The straightaways, which are so much easier to hit for most people, are much tougher kills. The backbone is between the gunner and the bird's vitals, and if you hold too low and don't break a wing, the bird can fly away packing an amazing amount of shot. Chances are he'll die before long, but chances are also that he won't end up in your game bag.

If you are bagging somewhere between two out of three and three out of four birds shot at, rest assured that you are among the elite of pheasant gunners. That kind of shooting, if you're taking just about everything in the way of makeable chances, is about as good as you're going to do year in and year out. Sure, there will be some years when you may have a season like I did in 1983 and kill nearly 90 percent of your intended victims. Steve Grooms once dropped forty-odd birds before one got away. But I wouldn't bet very much on that kind of success.

There are too many variables where game shooting in general is concerned, which is why champion trap and skeet gunners don't repeat their hundred-straights in the field. That's especially true with pheasants.

One problem with pheasants is that on occasion you'll encounter a rooster which refuses to acknowledge that he's dead. Although I've never had a bird do the classic "tower" described by many veteran grouse hunters—climbing almost vertically when hit and then dropping dead—I have had a number of birds die after flying several hundred yards.

Tom Huggler and I were hunting a large tract of set-aside ground several years ago. I'd taken a rooster and Tom had done some damage to a covey of quail on the east side of the road. Crossing the gravel to work the west side, we decided to split up because of the nature of the cover. Rebel and I headed north along a fence with a wide strip of dense grass on either side.

Several draws ran down to our fence line from the west. Rebel turned up the first one, very clearly making game. She pointed and relocated several times. On her fifth stop or so, a rooster flushed about 20 yards dead ahead of me.

Just as I touched off my right barrel, the bird climbed sharply to clear a cottonwood branch. Feathers flew, but I was just low enough to fail to drop the bird. I was about to follow up with a second shot when another rooster flushed to my left, much closer than the first. I switched gears, swung on him, and rocked him hard with the modified barrel.

Like the first bird, rooster number two kept on going. I

cursed my luck but kept my eye on the bird because I knew he was hit. Sure enough, a couple of hundred yards out, the bird seemed to lose control of his wings and dropped hard.

As long as the bird didn't run, he had few opportunities to hide—he was flying over very short grass pasture. Even though every bird I've seen drop like that was dead on the spot, I don't believe in taking chances with pheasants. Rebel and I went after the bird on the double.

The bird was right where it fell. I lifted it high into the air and yelled to catch Tom's attention. He and his setter, Macbeth, were working a good-looking draw below the hill where the bird had fallen. I signaled him to do an about-face and come back with me along the strip Rebel and I had started on. Tom swung Beth around.

My bird had nearly made it to the west boundary fence of the property we were hunting. I decided to follow that fence, at least until I got as far as the draw where we'd flushed the pair of roosters.

I was giving serious consideration to heading back down the draw, a good hundred yards of which we hadn't covered, when we reached the point where it intersected the fence. I looked for Reb to change directions and spotted her pointing straight into the fence. She'd located the first rooster, which had made it that far, and was lying breast up just on the opposite side of the barbed wire.

That's one experience I've never forgotten. It's my only double on pheasants, and we recovered the first half of it on pure blind luck. I could have lost the second bird as well, had I not kept my eyes on it. Watch birds you've shot at, especially those you know you've hit, until they are out of sight.

How can you become more effective at shooting pheasants? Like any other physical activity, wing shooting requires practice. Whether you go to a trap or skeet range, or whether you and a few of your buddies toss some birds with a hand trap, do a bit of shooting before the season starts.

How much practice you need depends on you. I'm not blessed with even average coordination, and if you are, you probably need less of it than I do.

Other game birds are, of course, excellent warm-ups for roosters. In most places, the pheasant season opens later than some other species, whether they be grouse, woodcock, quail, or doves. In my own case, I always try to take about a week to hunt woodcock somewhere I'm likely to find a lot of birds. There are

obvious differences between timberdoodles and ringnecks, but
there are enough similarities to make it worthwhile. Besides, my
dogs like it, and I'm not about to delay my bird shooting until the
first of November.

Preserves can be good tune-ups as well. However, I'm not
crazy about preserve pheasants. Either they are too easy or else
they act too much like wild birds and sneak or fly away. I hate to
see that when I'm paying good money for my birds.

I much prefer shooting quail or chukar on preserves. Both
are much more likely to hold for your dogs, and if they do
manage to escape, it's usually through a hail of shot. They're also
a good bit cheaper than pheasants, so you end up getting a lot
more shooting for your money, even if it isn't at ringnecks.

Another way to make yourself a better shot is to hunt with a
good dog. We'll go into this subject in much more detail a bit later
on, but briefly, dogs help you in several ways. They will let you
know that birds are around, will either point them or flush them
(hopefully, in range!), and will find a few dead birds and a lot of
cripples which would otherwise go unrecovered. Even though I
grew up hunting dogless, I'd just about as soon leave my gun
home as my dogs nowadays.

"Always anticipate the flush" is an extremely valuable piece
of advice offered by my friend Dave Prine. In other words, hunt in
a perpetual state of readiness. Another of Brown's Rules of
Pheasant Hunting says that a rooster is almost certain to flush
just when you least expect it.

Good dogless hunters may actually have a bit of an edge
here. Although they don't have that all-powerful canine nose to
alert them to birds, they also are less likely to be caught off guard
simply because the dog isn't making game. And sometimes, due
to wind direction or just to the vagaries of scent, even the best
dog will fail to detect a bird.

Several years ago, I opened the season with Mike Carroll,
Jerry Fagle, and Dick Downy. We were hunting in southern
Keokuk County, where Dick lives. Jake and I had split off from
the other three, who were hunting behind Dick's big yellow Lab,
Duke. By the time I reached our rendezvous point, the other
three had cased their guns, kenneled Duke, and were taking a
break next to Dick's ancient Jeep.

I broke the Sauer as I came up the gravel road to meet them.
Jake wasn't making game, and I figured that it was time for us to
take a breather, too.

Jake was off relieving himself in the far ditch as the four of us discussed where to go next. A cheeky ringneck took advantage of our distraction, flushing out of the near ditch not 10 yards from us. I was the only one with a gun ready at hand, and although it was still loaded, I was so startled that I couldn't coordinate closing the action and swinging on the bird while he was still in range.

Jake, who very seldom missed birds, regained interest quickly. Fifty yards farther down his side of the road, he pointed. This time, with the dog to give me advance notice, I managed to get it together and put the bird in the bag.

The final key to more successful pheasant shooting is the proper choice of shotshell load to match the gauge and choke gun that you shoot. That decision can be a good deal more complex than you may think, and is the subject of the next chapter.

Shooting Pheasants II

N the last chapter, I discussed guns for pheasant hunting and how to hit the birds. Outside of giving you my opinion that a pheasant hunter should use nothing smaller than a 20, I intentionally deferred all discussion of gauge, choke, and shotshell load to this chapter. My reason is simple: the three factors have to be considered together. All too often, outdoor writers are guilty of giving fragmented advice in this critical area. Is the 12 gauge the best gun for pheasants? Does a modified choke outperform the other choices? Are high-velocity 6s the best shotshell load? These questions are frequently answered separately, when in fact they are all interrelated.

Let's begin by getting rid of some myths concerning gauge and choke. Gauge doesn't tell you much except the relative size of the hole at the business end of your shotgun. It is a measurement which was arrived at in black powder days by determining how large a solid lead ball would fit into various shotgun barrels. If the barrel would accommodate a solid ball weighing ¹⁄₁₂ pound, it was designated a 12 gauge; ¹⁄₂₀ pound, 20 gauge, etc. The .410 is the only oddball here, and that is because it is a true caliber—like a rifle or a pistol—rather than a gauge.

As I said, gauge is immaterial to a certain extent, because it is what comes out of the barrel, and how it comes out, which is important—not the size of the barrel. You can shoot light 1-ounce loads in a 12, just as you can push heavy 1¼-ounce loads out of a 3-inch 20 gauge. But all in all, because of its larger bore diameter, the 12 has the capacity to put out more shot than does the 20.

Matching the proper load to your gun and to your specific hunting conditions can mean a limit of birds, even late in the year.

However, this does not mean that a 12 throws a bigger pattern than does a 20. This is where choke comes in.

Choke was developed by gunsmiths in the late nineteenth century. Both the Americans and the British take credit for the discovery. Simply put, choke is a small degree of constriction at the end of the bore which causes a shotgun to pattern tighter—and thus be effective at longer ranges—than if there were no constriction.

Prior to the discovery of choke and its effects on shotgun patterns, all shotguns were made without bore constriction, that is, with what is now called true cylinder choke. (This is a misnomer, because cylinder choke is in fact the absence of any choke at all.) Adding choke to a barrel increased the effective range of the shotgun considerably—an important consideration to hunters, especially duck shooters, in the late nineteenth century.

Since its inception, choke has been more or less standardized by shotgun manufacturers. It is determined in two ways. The first is the amount of constriction at the end of the barrel. The second, and the one of importance to hunters, is the percentage of shot the gun will place inside a circle 30 inches in diameter at 40 yards (table 1). Those figures were apparently arrived at in somewhat arbitrary fashion, but they've survived the test of time. Shotgun choke is evaluated the same way now as it was a century ago.

Table 1: Choke as determined by pattern percentage

Cylinder or skeet 1	40%
Improved cylinder or skeet 2	50
Modified	60
Improved modified	65
Full	70

It is choke which plays the key role in determining the size of a pattern, not gauge. If a full choke 12 puts 70 percent of its pellets into that magic 30-inch circle at 40 yards, then its pattern is no larger than that of a full choke 20, which should produce the same percentage.

In theory, that's the way things should work. Of course, you have to compare apples to apples. Using standard 2¾-inch high-velocity shells—such as Remington Express, Winchester Super-X, or Federal Hi-Power—and the same size shot, a pattern should be the same size from a full choke 12 as it is from a full choke 20. But there will be a difference in pattern density. In the ammunition I've specified, the standard 12 gauge load is 1¼ ounces of shot, while the 20 throws only 1 ounce. Size 6 shot, at about 225 pellets to the ounce, gives the 12 an advantage of better than 50 pellets to start with. These extra pellets, however, add to the density of the pattern rather than to its size, making it effective at longer ranges.

This is the theoretical relationship of choke and gauge. If you have guns of different gauges but the same choke, you can check it out yourself on a patterning board. If you do, you will learn why I used the word "theory" here. Bob Brister chose the title for his classic book, *Shotgunning: The Art and the Science,* for a very good reason. There are probably equal amounts of art and science to shotgunning, and what should happen when worked out mathematically is seldom what does happen when you go to the patterning board.

It has been said that it is as important for shotgunners to pattern their scatterguns as it is for rifle shooters to sight in. This is somewhat of an overstatement. Rifle shooters literally can miss the broad side of a barn if they do not sight in, especially with a badly aligned scope. Because the shotgun is a short-range weapon, and because of the margin for error its pattern allows, you won't ever be that far off.

Nevertheless, patterning is an extremely valuable exercise. It will show you a number of things: whether your gun shoots where you point it, whether it in fact delivers patterns consistent with the choke marked on the barrel, and which shot size and load perform best in your particular gun.

Shotgunning is much less precise than rifle shooting, because you are talking about hundreds of projectiles instead of just one, and they are being scattered around in a more or less random fashion. With a rifle, it is possible to put shots in nearly the same spot, time after time. With a shotgun, producing the same pattern twice is a virtual impossibility.

What you need to look for on the patterning board is an even distribution of shot, a pattern without a lot of gaping holes or clustering. You also want to look for repeated consistency with the same load. For this reason, you need to pattern the same load at least three times to see if it is giving you even performance on a consistent basis.

But let's start by evaluating your gun's choke. You want to find if it really is giving you a tight, full choke pattern (if that's what you want) or the more open pattern of an improved cylinder. In order to do this, you need to know not only the percentages different chokes are supposed to deliver—which I gave you in table 1—but also the number of pellets in your load so you can accurately arrive at that percentage. Table 2 gives you those figures for the most popular shot sizes used on pheasants and for all loads you're likely to use.

Table 2: Number of pellets in various pheasant loads

Shot number	Ounces of shot						
	3/4	7/8	1	1 1/8	1 1/4	1 3/8	1 1/2
4	101	118	135	152	169	186	203
5	127	149	170	191	213	234	255
6	169	197	225	253	281	309	338
7 1/2	263	303	350	397	444	492	525

Source: Figures courtesy of Winchester.
Note: Number of shot will vary slightly per ounce, with hard shot having a few more pellets and soft shot a few less.

Now all you need to do is shoot a few patterns with your gun, remembering to pattern it at least three times with the same load. Count the holes, divide the totals in table 2 into your count, and you will arrive at a percentage figure. This will give you a better idea of whether your gun is really throwing modified patterns out of that barrel that just happens to be stamped "modified."

Don't expect to come out right on the money. A full choke may throw 75 percent patterns with certain loads and shot sizes, and 65 percent patterns with others. You may have even more variation than this. There are several reasons for these deviations from the standard percentages.

The first reason is that gun manufacturers use slightly different bore constrictions and slightly different methods of choke boring. I can just about guarantee you that two guns of the same gauge and choke, made by two different companies, will throw very different pattern percentages using the very same shells. That's why you have to try different loads and even different brands of ammunition. You may find that a Remington Express 12 gauge load, 6 shot, 3¾-drams equivalent, and 1¼ ounces of shot, patterns differently from a Winchester Super-X or a Federal High Brass Classic with the same load and shot size.

Another problem is that there have been significant advances in shotshell design in recent years. If you hunt with a pre–World War II gun like I do—and there are still plenty of old doubles and Model 12s from that era being used—you may find that your old blunderbuss marked "modified" is throwing full choke patterns with new ammo. Modern shells are, in general, a lot better than what was available when your gun was made fifty years ago.

Another reason that your percentage may be off is pellet count. The figures I gave you are average. A few years back, I used to make up my own reloads of copper 6s for my 16 gauge— 3¼ drams equivalent, 1⅛ ounces of shot. When comparing them to Winchester Super-X lead loads, I found my own patterns were actually more open, whereas I expected them to be tighter with the harder copper shot. I found the reason when I compared the actual pellet count in one of my reloads to a Winchester factory load. The factory shell had 250 pellets, almost exactly what it should have had. Mine was so much lower than that, I couldn't believe it. But after checking three of my reloads, I discovered they were averaging only about 220 pellets—less than I should have gotten from a 1-ounce load of 6s.

Although it may seem disturbing to you that patterning and choke are so inexact, you can actually make it work to your advantage. For example, if you want tighter patterns, try using shells with copperplated, buffered shot, such as Winchester Double-X Magnums or Federal Premiums. The harder, buffered shot deforms less, giving tighter patterns in most guns. Regular lead loads will give more open patterns, which is what you may want for closer shots.

There is another factor which must be mentioned before we get away from patterning and theories and go on to what works best in the field. That is the third dimension of a pattern, or shot string.

What you see on the patterning board is a two-dimensional representation of a three-dimensional pattern. A pattern not only spreads out over space but also over time. Not all the pellets strike the target simultaneously. This time dimension is referred to as shot string.

Probably the main culprit in shot string is pellet deformation. Deformed pellets are not as efficient and therefore move slower than pellets which remain round. Deformed pellets also tend to veer off target.

Hard pellets deform less than soft ones, and large shot deforms less than small shot. Also, everything else being equal, the larger the gauge, the less deformation you get.

What shot string means to the hunter is that, especially on-long-range crossing shots, the load may string out sufficiently so that the tail-end pellets fail to reach the target on time. It may not make the difference between a hit and a miss, but it can cause the difference between a cripple and a kill.

Although the importance of shot string can be overstated, it is most definitely a factor which must be considered when evaluating patterns. If you don't believe it, read what Bob Brister has to say about it in *Shotgunning: The Art and the Science.* He had his wife tow targets behind the family station wagon to graphically demonstrate shot string. (For that undertaking, Brister deserves a medal for perseverance and his wife one for bravery under fire!)

But enough about theory and patterning. Let's apply all of this to bagging pheasants in the field.

The British, in their driven shoots, kill more pheasants than we could ever imagine. For those hunters in Great Britain who have the pounds to spend on driven pheasant shooting, it is possible for an individual shooter to kill more birds in a single day than a hard-core American hunter living in a top pheasant state can kill in a season. This is in no way a commercial for the big bucks driven pheasant shoots. All I am saying is that there are some fortunate English hunters who kill unbelievable numbers of birds.

This fact was even more true in the late nineteenth and early twentieth centuries, when the ringneck was just getting established on this side of the Atlantic. Back then, it was not unusual for an English sporting gentleman to kill thousands of pheasants in a single season. The Marquis of Ripon, who died in 1923 after a day afield during which he shot fifty-one grouse, killed nearly a quarter of a million pheasants in his lifetime!

Out of this period of extraordinarily prolific pheasant shoots come the writings of one Major Burrard, who applied a good bit of cold, hard English logic to the subject of pheasant shooting.

Burrard determined that a pheasant offered about 35 square inches of target area to the shooter, approximately half of which was vital area—those parts of the bird's body where a hit is likely to result in a kill. From examining a lot more dead birds than I've been able to autopsy, he determined that three hits to this vital area, assuming pellets with sufficient penetration, would result in a reasonably certain kill. His choice was British 6 shot, which is a bit smaller than American 6 shot. It equates fairly closely to our number 7 shot, which has almost disappeared except in loadings offered by some custom cartridge companies.

Other expert opinions are fairly similar. Jack O'Connor suggested a minimum of four to five hits with 6s. Francis Sell felt that it took six to eight hits to be certain of a clean kill.

Most of the experts specify a minimum amount of energy per pellet. For example, Bob Bell, in his excellent pheasant book, *Hunting the Long-Tailed Bird,* recommended three hits in the vital area, each hit requiring a minimum of 1¼ foot-pounds of energy.

A basic rule of shotgunning is that you use the smallest possible shot size which will give you adequate penetration. The smaller the shot, the denser the pattern. The denser the pattern, the more hits on the target. Hence the logic of using the smallest shot which will do the job.

While penetration is a bit difficult to measure, retained energy is not. Theories on necessary retained energy for effective kills on pheasants range from a low of Bell's 1¼ foot-pounds to a high of 1¾ foot-pounds. Table 3 compares retained energy of various shot sizes at 40 yards.

Table 3: Retained energy of shot at 40 yards

Shot size	Retained energy (foot-pounds)
4	4.3
5	3.2
6	2.3
7½	1.3

Note: Average velocity assumed.

Table 3 makes it easy to see why 6 shot is such a popular choice, and why it is so often recommended. It has plenty of retained energy at 40 yards, and in fact well beyond that distance. The next smaller size readily available, 7½, is at best borderline at 40 yards.

Does that mean that 6s are the load of choice? Let's not jump ahead so quickly. That load of 6s is the smallest shot size which will be effective at 40 yards, which is on the long side as far as pheasant shots go. But remember what I said earlier—that a specific load has to be related to a particular gauge and a particular choke. (Critics might even go so far here as to say that it needs to be related to a particular gun, given the peculiarities of shotguns!) Before we make that determination, let's go through one more mathematical exercise. This one will help you relate patterns to their potential effect on birds in the field.

A circle with a 30-inch diameter has an area of about 707 square inches. If you divide this by the 35 square inches of a pheasant's body area, you see that our 40-yard target covers an area equal to that of twenty pheasants—or, if you prefer, the truly vital area of forty pheasants.

What kind of pellet count will give you a very high probability of kills, given these statistics? Steve Grooms, in his book *Modern Pheasant Hunting*, settles on a figure of eighty-five hits, which I think is too low. That would be an average of four hits per bird, which should give two in the vital area. However, it does not leave sufficient margin for error to account for shot string, nor does it take into consideration the fact that all patterns are going to have at least some degree of unevenness.

Being a lover of round numbers, I've arrived—rather unscientifically—at one hundred as the pellet count I deem necessary for a pattern to be truly effective on pheasants. This will give an average of five hits per bird, or two to three in the vital area. Because I feel that three is none too many, and because I certainly don't want to take a chance on only a single vital hit, I

think that the figure of one hundred is a good, conservative minimum. Besides, it makes pellet counting much easier!

I also like what happens when I relate that figure back to the
various shot charges. I find that 1 ounce of 6s, the standard high-
velocity 20 gauge load, should put about 112 pellets in the circle
at 40 yards, if fired from an improved cylinder (IC) barrel, which
patterns 50 percent. This tells me that 40 yards is approaching
the maximum range for that particular combination, which is
verified by what I've experienced in the field.

It also tells me that anything smaller than a 20 gauge is not a
good choice for pheasants, unless you want to restrict yourself to
less than 40-yard shots. The 28 gauge, for example, will put just
over one hundred pellets in the circle with its standard ¾-ounce
load from a modified barrel that throws a 60 percent pattern. The
problem is, most 28s are open choked in single-barrel guns, or
are offered as IC-modified combinations in doubles. Thus, even
with a double, unless you have the presence of mind to go to the
tighter barrel for the first shot, you are treading on thin ice if you
have a bird that flushes at long range. Although my experience
with a 28 on pheasants is limited, I don't think it is a good choice
because it restricts you to a maximum range of less than 40
yards.

Armed with the knowledge of what it takes to deliver an effective pattern at 40 yards, we can finally begin to make some
logical decisions about the proper combination of gauge, choke,
and load. Let me add here that there is no magic about the 40-
yard range. You may want to have the capability of killing birds
beyond that mark. If so, simply pattern your gun at 45 or 50
yards, whatever you choose as an extreme limit for your shots.

Remember, however, that most hunters—myself included—
tend to overestimate range. Do you really kill all that many birds
beyond 40 yards? I know that I shoot many more birds at around
20 yards than I do at 40 or beyond. I also know that I don't
consider myself a good enough shot to consistently center birds
much beyond 40 yards. And I'm not interested in crippling
pheasants to benefit the fox population.

Returning to the choice of choke, let's assume that you are
going to go out and buy a new scattergun for pheasants. You've
already made your selection as far as make, model, barrel length,
and gauge are concerned. Now you're down to the question of
choke.

One easy way to solve the problem is to buy a gun with
screw-in chokes. These devices, although we tend to think of

them as new, have really been around for some time. The Poly-Choke, for example, has certainly survived the test of time and is still seen quite often in the field.

There really isn't much difference between the newer, screw-in models and the old Poly-Choke. Of course, the screw-in variety is prettier—it doesn't make your gun look like something Elliot Ness used when he was after Al Capone. It can also be used on doubles, whereas the Poly-Choke could not.

However, the old Poly-Choke has one advantage over the choke tubes: it is adjustable. You can change your choke simply by giving it a twist. Screw-in chokes require that you dig out a wrench and a new tube to make a switch.

But there are definite advantages to having a selection of chokes available. When the birds are sitting tight, you use a more open choke. On those days we all hate to think about, when the roosters are wearing their Nikes and flushing way ahead, you use a tighter choke.

The problem is that you don't always know how the birds are going to behave. After a couple or three wild flushes, you may decide it's time to twist the Poly-Choke to full or to hunt for the wrench and another tube. About the time you do that, Brown's Law of Pheasant Unpredictability says that the odds are in favor of the next rooster coming up in your face.

When I use my old Sauer with fixed chokes, I find myself faced with a similar problem on mixed-bag pheasant and quail hunts. If I start with pheasant loads in the gun, I can almost guarantee that my first action will come on a covey of bobwhites. I switch to the low-brass 8s to hunt the singles and immediately encounter a rooster. I've almost decided I'd be better off shooting one or the other rather than fumbling around to change shells. And that's relatively easy to do with a double. I can't imagine doing it with a repeater.

In other words, there's something to be said for going with what you have and not trying to alter your choke or load. However, it is valuable to have the capability to change chokes, as long as you don't overdo it. I started out with the rather odd combination of IC and full tubes in my SKB, then switched to an even more unusual skeet and modified. With the exception of one December hunt, I didn't change chokes the rest of the season.

Along with the rule of using the smallest size shot which will do the job, there is, or should be, a rule which says that you should use the most open choke which will provide effective patterns. The reason is, as stated earlier, that the more open choke throws a bigger pattern. This does two things for the hunter: it gives more margin for error in shooting, and it reduces the possibility of badly shot-up game at close range. I think most pheasant hunters are in favor of both points.

We've already determined that an improved cylinder 20 gauge, shooting a 1-ounce load of 6s, will produce an effective 40-yard pattern. Obviously, then, the standard 1⅛-ounce and 1¼-ounce loads in the 16 and 12 gauges, respectively, will be effective at even longer ranges. In a 50 percent IC barrel, the 16 will deliver about 125 pellets in the circle, and the 12 about 140. That's certainly plenty of killing power.

One might even argue the case for going to a more open choke in 12 gauge. However, that would mean cylinder, or skeet 1. This choke is normally found only on slug barrels, or on the first barrel of a double made for skeet shooters. Most hunters would probably be uncomfortable with anything as short as a slug barrel. As to doubles designed for skeet shooting, they tend to be a good bit heavier than field models and may be more than a pheasant hunter wants to carry afield, especially in 12 gauge.

What you can do with a 12 gauge, even with as open a choke as improved cylinder, is to go to a 1-ounce load. This will reduce recoil while still giving you plenty of pellets at 40 yards, and far fewer at closer ranges where they will only do more damage to the meat. The problem comes in finding a quality 1-ounce 12 gauge load. The British use it a lot. We don't. And if you start buying the bargain variety shells, you'll be getting softer pellets. At 40 yards, you may no longer have an effective pattern.

Another possibility for making the pattern less dense is to go to a size larger shot. One and one-fourth ounces of 5s, for example, should give about 107 pellets in the circle at 40 yards—still quite effective. Fives also offer the advantage of additional energy, and therefore greater penetration.

In summary, IC is the choke to choose if you're selecting a pheasant gun. It will deliver killing patterns in 12, 16, and 20 gauge guns with standard loads. It has a more open, and therefore less damaging, pattern at ranges up to 40 yards. Ballistics research also tells us that an IC pattern opens quicker than either a modified or full choke, again meaning that it's a better choice for close shots.

But what do you do if you inherited grandad's full choke 12 gauge Model 12? Do you hang it on the wall and rush out to buy another gun? I don't think I would—at least not without trying to adapt that fine piece of work to modern pheasants.

First, I'd pattern it with a variety of loads, at which point I might well find that it patterns even more than 70 percent with modern shells. If that is the case, I would seriously consider having a reliable gunsmith open the choke for me. This is a relatively simple and inexpensive operation.

What if you don't want to do that? If you reload, there are a couple of possibilities. One is to whip up a batch of 1-ounce loads using hard shot. My choice would be copperplated 6s. Another is to stick with the standard 1¼-ounce load but use the Polywad Spred-R. This is a little plastic device which, when inserted into your load, will deliver 50 percent patterns from a full choke barrel. I've tried it and it works. The patterns are not only opened considerably, but they are quite even as well.

With the exception of using the Spred-R, you are going to have to live with one undeniable fact: that full choke is going to throw much smaller and much tighter patterns than an IC or modified gun. If you don't reload, there isn't much you can do to make the pattern bigger. However, there is a simple solution to make it less dense.

Although we said 6 shot is the smallest size practical for pheasants under most circumstances, it certainly isn't the only shot which will kill birds out to 40 yards. I've already suggested the possibility of using 5s, even in a 12 choked improved cylinder. The same logic should be used with your full choke gun.

Fives, in a 1¼-ounce load, will deliver about 150 pellets from a 70 percent barrel in our test pattern. That's very lethal. Even using 4s, you should get about 120 hits in the 30-inch circle. You should keep in mind also that a full choke tends to pattern better with larger shot sizes—not to mention the fact that you run much less risk of producing instant pheasant hamburger if you take a shot at 25 yards.

The solution to the problem of gauge, choke, and load, then, is a relatively simple one. You want an effective pattern at long range, yet something which will leave you more than a pile of feathers at close range. Table 4, which gives the pellet strikes in a 30-inch circle at 40 yards for various gauges, chokes, and loads should help you make the match which will produce an effective combination.

Table 4 finally gets us where we wanted to go at the beginning of the chapter. It tells us, for example, that a load of 5s works fine in the modified barrel of my 16 gauge double, but that the same load would be a bit thin from my IC barrel at 40 yards. I've confirmed that on my own pattern boards and in the field.

Table 4: Hits in 30-inch circle (40 yards) by gauge, choke, shot size

Gauge	Choke	Shot size		
		4	5	6
12 (1¼ oz load)	IC	85	107	140
	Modified	102	128	169
	Full	119	149	197
16 (1⅛ oz load)	IC	76	95	126
	Modified	91	121	152
	Full	106	134	177
20 (1 oz load)	IC	67	85	112
	Modified	81	102	135
	Full	94	119	157

Note: Choke assumes IC at 50 percent, modified at 60 percent, full at 70 percent.

But if 6s are effective from a modified 16 gauge barrel, and if the pattern is not too dense (which it almost certainly is not, given that it is my second shot), why would I want to use 5s? The answer comes more in gut feeling, more in the "art" end of shotgunning, than in the science, and in a desire to give myself added penetration on late-season birds.

By the end of the year, those pheasants which were perhaps only five months old when you shot at them on opening day now have a couple of months additional maturity and considerably more exposure to hunters. They're a bit bigger, and flushes are likely to be wilder.

The last bird of the 1984 season is a perfect example of my point. Tom Huggler and I were finishing up a four-day hunt which, to say the least, had been less than spectacular. It was a below average year for Iowa pheasants. The weather was cold but dry, with no heavy snow to push the birds into thick cover where they might hold.

Tom was on a fence line, while I worked a creek. The action was slow until he pushed a big cock back in my direction. The bird was angling slightly away from me, quite a ways out, but offering me an excellent view as he crossed from left to right.

I had time to think about it and went to my back trigger. I swung with the big rooster and watched him bounce a couple of times as he hit the frozen plowing. He never twitched a feather.

Later that evening, when I cleaned the bird, I was amazed to find that my copper 5s were lying between the skin and the breast, on the bird's left side. Then I remembered that I'd hit him from the right. At a range of about 40 yards, give or take 5 either way, those 5s had passed completely through the bird's body. I couldn't believe it but confirmed it by turning the bird over and looking at the entry wounds. That's the kind of stopping power I like to have on late-season birds.

Of course, a lot depends on shot placement and range. A bird from the 1987 season brought that point home to me very clearly.

Things weren't going especially well for me that day. Birds were jumping at the fringe of effective range, which happened to be mostly out of effective range for the way I was shooting. I'd succeeded in scratching one down, which Heidi had recovered. We'd also lost another when I dropped one rooster from a group of ten or twelve that flushed from a weedy creek bottom. The bird wasn't hit all that hard from the way it dropped. Heidi was in her first year on pheasants, and she just couldn't sort out the right trail amongst all that pheasant scent. I was much more upset with myself than with her.

By the time we turned around to head back to the car, clear at the other end of the section, I was down to half a dozen quail loads. I had started with about the same number of pheasant loads and had used them up, mostly in wasted effort, except for the one bird in my vest. I was kicking myself in the rear not only for losing a cripple but for forgetting to swap the quail loads for some 6s before I went to an area which I knew didn't have any bobwhites.

Outside of a relatively bare fencerow, the only cover to walk back on was the same creek we'd just followed. However, it was fairly wide and deep. Hope springs eternal, and I thought that there might still be a bird on the far side which hadn't flushed on our way up the creek.

Although Heidi worked the cover well, she didn't show much indication of pheasant scent. Suddenly, within about 200 yards of the car, she locked on in some heavy weeds just over the lip of the creek bank. Had to be a hen sitting that tight, I told myself.

The bank was very steep, and I knew that if I tried to get down to flush the bird, I'd probably be in at best a poor position for the shot. I picked up a clod of dirt from the field bordering the creek and threw it into the weeds.

The rooster erupted right under Heidi's nose. Using those light loads of 8s, I knew I shouldn't waste much time. I hammered the bird as it rose to clear the far bank. Feathers flew as if someone had tossed a pillow into the air. I congratulated myself and skidded down the bank after Heidi.

It took the young shorthair a bit of time to get down our side and up the other, and me even more. Although I hadn't thought there was any need for haste and expected to find Heidi on the other side with the bird, I wanted to be sure, having lost one cripple already.

Heidi found the spot where the bird had hit in an open, combined soybean field. I was surprised he wasn't still there, but I expected her to track him back to the creek and dig him out of the weeds, where I figured his dying effort had taken him.

Although we searched long and hard, we never did find that bird. I pride myself on not losing cripples, which made that one of the unhappiest days in my experience as a pheasant hunter. It's the only time I've ever lost 2 birds in the same day. Considering that over the entire span of time from 1981 to 1987 I bagged 205 pheasants and only lost 7, 2 in one day was a real disaster.

Reflecting on it after the hunt, however, the reasons for losing the second cripple became more apparent. Heidi had all of two weeks' experience on pheasants at that point. She is now an excellent cripple dog but was still very much a student of the game at that time.

More importantly, I was shooting a light load of 8s. Although I took the shot at under 25 yards, the bird was going dead away—the toughest kind of chance for a kill. Unless you hit the head, you have to drive the shot through the bird's back to reach its vital areas. I obviously broke at least one wing, but if those 8s made it to the bird's vitals, it was not with enough force left to produce an instant kill. Either the bird hit and ran like crazy—entirely possible, since I couldn't see it come down because of tall weeds—or it managed the few yards back to the creek bank and sat tight in the heavy cover. In any case, it was a lost bird, something which any real pheasant hunter knows is a possibility but hates to experience.

The moral of the story is that I don't trust light loads of small shot, even at close ranges. Although I've killed pheasants with quail loads, I'd rather use 5s than 8s if I have to make that choice. Small shot, even if lethal, also gives the bird cleaner, the cook, and the person trying to enjoy a meal of pheasant more lead to worry about.

Let's go back to table 4. Readers may wonder why I confined myself to the choice of standard high velocity loads for each gauge. Are these the only logical choices?

Certainly not. In addition to the possibility of using lighter loads for the 12—when you can find them in quality shells—there is also the option of using loads such as Federal Premiums, Winchester Double Xs, or Remington Nitro Magnums. All three are available in either 2¾-inch or 3-inch versions for the 12 and 20 gauges, and Winchester Double Xs can be had in 2¾ inches for the 16. Steve Grooms, an excellent pheasant hunter and one of the best shots I've ever seen, swears by the Federal Premiums out of his 12 gauge double, which is choked IC-modified.

My only word of caution is to suggest that you stick with the 2¾-inch option if you do decide to use these superefficient, tight patterning loads. That gives 20 gauge shooters one ounce loads using Federal Premiums or Remington Premiers. All three manufacturers also offer 2¾-inch short magnums, which pack an extra ⅛ ounce of shot over the standard long-range loads. I've had extremely good luck with Winchester's Double X Magnum in both 16 and 20 gauge.

The 3-inch magnum is a poor choice for pheasants. Although improvements have been made in 3-inch shells, it is difficult to make them as ballistically efficient as the 2¾-inch loads. By packing in too much shot, velocity and pattern tend to suffer. In particular, 20 gauge shooters should not be attracted by the siren song of matching a 12 gauge load by using a 3-inch 20. One and one-eighth ounces of shot in the short magnums works fine in a 20 and offers excellent stopping power on pheasants. With the 3-inch shells, you're asking for a sore shoulder for little or no gain out where it counts.

In fact, my new SKB with choke tubes and the short magnums has caused me to revise my thinking on choke and load. Using that unusual combination of skeet and modified chokes, I found that the Winchester XX load of 1⅛ ounces of copper 7½s was absolutely deadly on my first shot. That load packs nearly four hundred pellets, and matching that much shot with an open choke works very well. I seldom take my first shot at 40 yards, so I don't worry about whether I can get adequate penetration at that distance. I used a 1-ounce load of Federal Premium 6s in the modified barrel, which certainly gave me all the stopping power I needed at longer range.

I'm toying with the idea of using an IC choke in that second barrel with a 1⅛-ounce load of XX 6s. I have some patterning to do before I make that jump, but on paper it looks very effective, even beyond 40 yards.

I've saved one more possibility for last because it is a controversial choice. I'm referring, of course, to steel shot.

There are still a lot of waterfowlers who have very little good to say about steel. Unfortunately, they already have no choice in many areas and will be forced to use steel everywhere in the very near future.

Some states also require the use of steel for pheasants on certain areas, especially those used by large numbers of waterfowl. Those requirements are almost certain to increase in the future, although those of us who shoot old doubles fervently hope that we will not be faced with a total ban on lead shot.

The main problem with steel for ducks and geese is that it is lighter than lead and loses velocity, and therefore penetration, at extended ranges. This is much less of a problem for pheasant hunters. Tests have shown that steel works very well at least out to 40 yards, and even beyond. However, it does require a few adjustments.

Because steel is much harder than lead, there is much less pellet deformation. Patterns are going to be tighter. An improved cylinder is likely to throw 60–70 percent patterns—in other words, more like modified or full—with steel. You shouldn't use a tight choke.

As I suggested earlier, you should also avoid shooting steel in older guns, especially doubles. I'd also hesitate with a cherished Model 12, which is likely to have too much choke to shoot steel well at any rate. It's not going to hurt you, like shooting smokeless powder through a Damascus barrel, but it could well damage that valuable gun.

Because steel is lighter than lead, steel pellets of the same size occupy more space. For example, there are 135 lead 4s to an ounce, compared to 191 steel 4s. That means the ammunition makers can't fit as much steel into a given shell. You won't find a 2¾-inch 12 gauge shell which contains any more than 1¼ ounces of shot. This drops to ¹⁵/₁₆ and ¾ ounces for the 2¾-inch 16 and 20, respectively.

Remembering that steel patterns tighter, you need to select larger shot sizes. The usual recommendation for pheasants is steel 4s. The figure for an effective pattern still holds at one hundred hits, whether you're shooting lead or steel, so if you do go to steel, I suggest you do some patterning first. Many duck hunters who shoot it a lot, and who shoot at reasonable ranges, feel it is very effective. Some who have become accustomed to the way it performs also use it on pheasants, with very good results.

One final word of advice. For dogless hunters, or for those

who know they will fall victim to the temptation of taking shots beyond 40 yards, a combination which delivers more margin for error is called for. Such hunters may want to go with the 1½-ounce load in a 12 gauge, or with heavier loads or a tighter choke in a 20.

Even after testing various combinations on the patterning board, the real test will come when you try them out in the field. If what you're using delivers birds in the bag in fit condition for the table, you've got a winner.

The *Real* Pheasant Hunters

T its most basic level, pheasant hunting consists of three elements: finding birds, forcing them to flush in range, and putting them in the bag. All three of those elements can be rendered infinitely easier—not to mention more enjoyable—for the hunter who has the services of a decent pheasant dog.

I grew up hunting dogless, and my family and I, along with most other pheasant hunters of that era, put our share of birds in the freezer. Speaking for myself, however, a lot of those birds were shot on the ground. Speaking for many of my contemporaries, lots of their birds were taken in the famous cornfield drives, where dog work was at perhaps its greatest disadvantage, and where sheer manpower helped make up for the lack of canine support.

The Iowa DNR estimates that dogless hunters are likely to lose as many as three of every ten roosters they drop, whereas those with dogs will only lose one in ten. Being a skeptic when it comes to accepting other people's figures, and having the data base of my notebooks readily at hand, I decided to do my own survey on birds lost. I was surprised at the results.

From 1981 to 1988, I had the services of at least an average pheasant dog at all times. During those eight seasons, I bagged 235 roosters while losing 13. From my notes, I could clearly identify 42 retrieves as having been difficult, ones that in all likelihood I would not have made myself without a dog. In addition, my dogs retrieved 7 birds crippled by other hunters and not recovered. Since I wouldn't have found any of those without the

*Larry Brown's English pointer Jake, his first really
good pheasant dog, taught him how different it is to
hunt birds with canine assistance.*

dogs, I look at it as having a net loss of 6 birds over eight seasons.
But even figuring the 13 birds I knocked down and failed to recover, it comes out much closer to losing 1 bird out of 20, rather
than 1 out of 10.

Analyzing those 13 lost birds in more detail, I find that there
are good reasons why most of them escaped, and often it was not
really the dog's fault at all.

I lost a total of three roosters with Jake. One fell on the wrong
side of a hog wire fence and had a considerable head start by the
time I got the dog across. Jake actually took off on the trail of
another, but I hacked him back because I thought that I knew
more about it than he did. Again, that gave the bird too much of a
lead. I dropped the third in a very weedy cornfield, and not only
could Jake not find it, neither could two Labs that gave it their
best as well. All three converged on the spot where the bird fell
seconds after it hit. I still think the ground swallowed that bird.

Rebel lost two birds in her first season on pheasants, as did

Heidi. In Reb's case, she isn't as strong a retriever as I'd like. Heidi is much better, but one of her two losses dropped on the opposite bank of a steeply sided creek, and the other folded in a draw where at least a dozen pheasants had been holed up. Unraveling that cripple's scent was simply beyond her.

Another of my lost birds came with a hunting companion's Lab. Labs are generally ranked at or near the top as retrievers, and deservedly so. This one, however, hadn't had a lot of experience on pheasants. It was also a very cold day, when scenting is tough.

Four of my lost birds came in a single season—1988. I'm convinced that the extreme drought we suffered in Iowa was the culprit that year. Every hunter I know had the same experience. Dogs with excellent noses hunted as if they had the canine world's worst sinus cold. It was still preferable to hunting dogless, but dog work was certainly far below normal. When I stop to think about the little puffs of dust I raised every time I took a step through picked corn, I can understand why they had problems.

A brief morning hunt I made during the 1987 season is the perfect example of the importance of good retrieving to the pheasant hunter.

I was hunting a farm in northern Poweshiek County where I had permission to hunt three-quarters of the section—480 acres, which is a lot of territory to cover. Heidi and I started our efforts in picked corn. The weather was pleasant, clear skies and temperatures in the fifties, and I anticipated finding the birds in relatively light cover.

Sure enough, about fifteen minutes after we'd hit the corn, a rooster flushed wild ahead of me at the fringe of effective range. I dropped him, but he hit running. Fortunately, Heidi was not far behind. Picked corn lets a dog use its eyes as well as its nose, and Heidi ran the bird to ground before it could reach heavier cover.

After a couple of nice points and heart-stopping flushes from tight-sitting hens, we started our circle back to the car. We were working edge cover, where the picked corn ran up against a medium-sized creek with a fair strip of heavier cover on either bank. I let Heidi figure out where to hunt.

About 200 yards from the road where I'd parked, she dove into the heavy grass on the near bank and locked up. Another hen. I'd scarcely had time to relax when she tiptoed a few yards ahead and pointed again. This time, a gaudy rooster came straight up out of the weeds, streaming tailfeathers behind him and cackling his displeasure. The shot was a relatively easy one, and I marked his fall not far on the other side of the creek, still in the heavy cover. I strolled over in that direction, expecting Heidi to return me a dead bird.

When I saw Heidi shoot out the far side of the cover and head back in the direction we'd come from, I reached for my whistle to bring her back. But good sense prevailed for once, as I remembered those times when I'd called dogs off escaping birds. If the bird was in the heavy grass, it would probably still be there when the dog came back. If it was a runner, it would certainly get away if I called her off.

I crossed the creek and walked through the strip of heavy stuff to a pasture beyond it. I got there just in time to see Heidi dive back into the heavy cover. A few seconds later, she emerged with a rooster in her mouth—well over 100 yards away from where I'd marked that "dead" bird.

The moral of the story is quite clear. That hunt resulted in two birds in the bag with two shots fired. Without the dog's help, I doubt that I could have stopped the first runner in the corn with my second barrel, and I am positive that I would have lost the bird by the creek. I never even saw it run out the far side.

Of course, retrieving is only one of the three elements I mentioned at the start of the chapter. I began with it simply because it is by far the easiest to quantify from my notebooks. But I am firmly convinced, as are various game commissions and other organizations with access to significant data on the subject, that dogs will also help pheasant hunters find more birds in the first place, not to mention those cripples that they prevent from escaping.

Which breed of dog ranks at the top of the heap for a pheasant hunter? This is a difficult question. There is no one "right" choice of breeds, and there are about as many different opinions as there are on the choice of gauge, choke, and shotshell. But unlike with guns and loads, we can't really rely on facts and figures at all. What we have to go by is personal preferences and gut feelings.

I once gave some thought to devising a scale for evaluating the potential of various breeds as pheasant dogs. I thought about including such factors as range, retrieving ability, trainability, and tolerance for cold weather. I considered using a numerical scale of one to five for each category and adding the total score to come up with the best breed.

Unfortunately, this approach doesn't work very well. While one can make some accurate generalizations—such as Labs tolerate the cold much better than English pointers, and springer spaniels are better natural retrievers than English setters—there are too many differences between individual dogs of any given breed.

Even the decision of whether to go with a pointing or a flushing breed is a question of the individual hunter's preference. Both have advantages and disadvantages, as we will see shortly.

But I do want to put one long-standing myth to rest. The old bit of conventional wisdom that pointing dogs can't handle pheasants is simply not true.

From 1981 to 1988, my two English pointers, Jake and Rebel, and my German shorthair, Heidi, made over five hundred productive points on pheasants. About one hundred of those resulted in a pheasant in the bag. This means that somewhat fewer than half the birds I shot during those eight seasons were pointed. Given the unpredictable nature of pheasants, I rather expect that percentage is more or less normal for hunters who run decent pointing dogs.

Obviously, things would be a lot easier for the pointing dog owner if one could shoot hens as well as cocks. In general, hens run a lot less and therefore get pointed more. Of course, late in the season, when the ratio of hens to roosters has become quite skewed, one gets a much higher percentage of hen points than on opening day. I've had frustrating late-season hunts where my dogs have nailed over a dozen birds, none of them roosters.

The pheasant hunter needs to be a skeptic when it comes to generalizations about types or breeds of dogs and must especially be wary of people I refer to as "breed fanatics." Often these folks raise one particular breed of dog, and they have an obvious vested interest in convincing you, the potential buyer, that the curly coated pointing spaniel is clearly the finest pheasant dog ever developed.

There is no one breed which is as closely identified with pheasant hunting as is the English pointer with bobwhite quail or the English setter with ruffed grouse. This may be due to the fact that pheasants are hunted in such a wide variety of cover. It may also stem partially from the fact that the pheasant is a bit more of a "blue collar" bird than are either quail or grouse. The devotees of those two birds elevate their pursuit to an almost ethereal level. Pheasant hunting, on the other hand, has always had a bit more to do with putting meat on the table. Just as pheasant hunters have often grabbed whatever gun happened to be handy, they have also used whatever breed of dog they happened to own. Thus, a pointer bred and acquired to hunt quail or a Lab meant for waterfowling could both end up seeing double duty on pheasants.

How you hunt and where you hunt are key factors to consider when mulling over what kind of dog you should have. I've never owned a flushing dog and doubt that I ever will. Although I've hunted with some excellent ones, and although they outperform pointing dogs in many instances, I simply prefer to work with pointers. Because I hunt a wide variety of covers, I own two distinctly different dogs. Heidi is a slow, meticulous worker who will bust heavy cover all day, and who will work a narrow creek or a fence line slowly enough so that her owner can easily keep up. Rebel is much faster and is more at home where there is lots of lighter cover to hunt. Between the two, I have the best canine team I've ever owned.

Steve Grooms, who has hunted with several of my dogs, once remarked to me that I've owned animals which tend to be typical of their breeds. This is an accurate observation. Heidi works close, like German shorthairs are supposed to, and is an excellent retriever. Rebel isn't really a big-going dog for an English pointer, but she's a ground-burner compared to Heidi. She's also weaker in the retrieving department. Steve also saw me hunt with—or more accurately for—Nick, an Irish setter who didn't really belong in the field. Most of them don't.

But once again, let me caution you to beware of breed generalizations. There are many shorthairs which range out a lot more than the majority of pheasant hunters would find comfortable. And while I've yet to see a really close-working English pointer, Rebel's father, Jake, was deadly on cripples, often a weakness of the breed. Likewise, although I've never seen a good one in the field, I'm sure that there are some Irish setters that do a competent job on pheasants.

The problem with breed generalizations is that many of them are no more accurate than that bit of conventional wisdom about pointing dogs being unable to handle pheasants. They may apply to the breed as it was ten or twenty years ago, but not as it is today.

Nearly all of the "continental" breeds—the versatile pointing dogs which originated in Europe, such as the Brittany and the shorthair, to name the two most popular representatives—are now more clearly bird dogs than when they first arrived in this country. In Europe, they were, and still are, jacks-of-all-trades—in general, a bit on the slow and plodding side for the tastes of

American bird hunters. American breeders have changed that by breeding for faster, more stylish dogs. In some cases, I feel that their quest for speed has gone too far.

The Irish and the Gordon setters were once both excellent bird dogs. Now you will find far more representatives of both breeds in dog shows than in pheasant cover. Gordon people claim, however, that their breed has not developed distinct show and field strains. I once acted as gun at a Gordon fun trial which included a lot of dogs that had never hunted. I readily admit to being impressed by the fact that every dog I saw, when exposed to birds, exhibited decent natural ability. Two dogs which had considerable hunting experience could have run in a brace with either of the English pointers I've owned.

Some breeds that are well-known for hunting have a significant split in the "family tree" between field dogs and show dogs. Three examples that come to mind immediately are the English setter, springer spaniel, and golden retriever. All make fine pheasant dogs if you select an animal from a hunting line. On the other hand, there are lines within each which have been bred for the show ring for many generations.

Particularly in the case of English setters and springer spaniels, the split is so significant that it doesn't take a very discerning eye to tell a show dog from a hunting dog. Setters bred for show may be nearly twice as big as their hunting cousins. The difference is only slightly less pronounced where springers are concerned.

Owners of these dogs may tell you that they are excellent hunters, and they may believe every word of what they are saying, even if they never take their dogs to the field. After all, the breed description does say that these are sporting dogs.

Perhaps the best advice for those in the market for a dog is to go to a kennel with a reputation for producing good hunters. Better still, if you have a hunting companion whose dog you admire, find out where he or she got it. Chances are good that a dog from the same bloodlines will also be a good hunter. There is often nearly as much difference between bloodlines within breeds as there is between one breed and another. The only problem is that the difference isn't very apparent until you see both strains in the field. Be particularly cautious in the case of those breeds with distinct show and hunting strains.

Shooting preserves can be good places to go if you are looking for a hunting dog. Many of them breed their own hunting stock, and they often have more than one breed available to choose from. Chances are very good, because of the nature of their business, that they will not be breeding show dogs.

Unless you are particularly sold on one of the less common breeds, I would also suggest that you make your selection from what is popular in your area. Here in Iowa, Brittanies and short-hairs dominate among the pointing dogs. Labs are the clear leaders among the flushers, with quite a few springers and goldens around as well.

There are many other breeds that do a good job on ringnecks. In most places, you won't have much trouble finding an English pointer or setter from good breeding. Likewise, there are plenty of Chesapeakes around for those who fancy retrievers.

Among the lesser-known pointing breeds, Gordon setters and drahthaars have a small but loyal following. If they strike your fancy, be aware that there are far fewer litters available and that pups will cost you about twice what you'd pay for the more popular breeds. The same is true with Boykin and American water spaniels. Hunting cockers are also starting to reappear, but they also are quite rare and relatively expensive, and the vast majority of the breed is show stock.

While I've said that the offspring of show champions probably aren't the best candidates for hunting dogs, I should also warn you that field trial titles in the family tree are not necessarily the best recommendation either. Among other illustrious ancestors in Jake and Rebel's family is Paladin's Royal Flush, winner of the National Pheasant Championship. Although that may sound like an excellent recommendation for a pheasant dog, the title is the result of a field trial where the judges follow the dogs on horseback. Tagging along behind those two pointers, there are definitely times I've wished for a horse. Most pheasant hunters would be less than satisfied with pheasant dogs that hunt that fast and that far out. I lived with it because of their excellent noses, but I also did my best to slow them down a lot.

Championships in standard retriever trials also mean little to the pheasant hunter. These are strictly retrieving affairs, striving to develop dogs of very high intelligence but which are extremely reliant on commands from their handlers. This does not encourage the kind of get-out-and-beat-the-brush independence that a hunter wants a bird finder to possess.

On the other hand, trials run by the National Shoot to Retrieve Association (NSTRA) for the pointing breeds approximate hunting conditions about as well as possible. Likewise, more realistic field trials are being developed for retrievers. If a breeder advertises "field trial champion bloodlines," ask what kind of trials. Also, tell the breeder what kind of dog you're looking for. Reputable breeders don't want to sell you the wrong dog any more than you want to buy one. Their reputation and success depend on satisfied customers.

As I mentioned earlier, the flushing versus pointing dog controversy is impossible to settle. Let's start with the flushers and take a quick look at advantages and disadvantages of the major breeds, as well as the typical differences between them. As you ponder these characteristics, remember what I said about breed generalizations and how inaccurate they can be. The ones I mention are those I've observed in dogs with which I've hunted.

The flushing breeds are all very good natural retrievers, which is a real plus for a pheasant hunter. If all you want is a dog that will find birds in range and put them into the air for you, training isn't very hard. All the dog needs to know is what a pheasant smells like and that it needs to hunt within gun range.

Of the flushing breeds, only the spaniels were actually bred for upland hunting. Retrievers were meant to do just that—fetch from land or water. Although good upland hunting strains have been developed, especially among Labs and goldens, there are other individuals that almost have to be taught how to hunt.

The springer is the real hunting dynamo of the more popular flushing breeds, and the Lab is probably at the other end of the scale. You are more likely to have to lean on a springer to get it to stay in range, and to encourage a Lab to get out and hunt more. I'll add, however, that I've seen several Labs that ranged out more than a flushing dog should.

All flushing breeds come well equipped to handle very cold weather, which is an important consideration in most of the pheasant's range. In fact, Labs and Chesapeakes will probably go outside and frolic when you have absolutely no desire to stray from the hearth.

Among the pointing breeds, English pointers and English setters have the best noses. They also cover the most ground. That is why they win all the major horseback field trials. They will probably find birds faster than other breeds, but those birds may well have departed by the time you reach the dog.

Most pointers and setters do not retrieve naturally. You must convince them to find the bird you've just shot before they can go on and find another one for you. The English pointer also has a low tolerance for cold. People who use these breeds on pheasants do so mainly because they are super bird finders and make

Steve Grooms's hard-charging springer spaniel, Brandy, shows that a barbed wire fence won't keep her from the birds.

breathtaking points. "Statue" has become a cliche for a dog on point, but it was undoubtedly the result of some writer seeing a pointer or setter locked up on birds.

The continental or versatile breeds tend to produce good natural retrievers. They cover less ground and work closer to the hunter than do pointers and setters. Cold weather hunting isn't much of a problem for Brittanies, and drahthaars are probably the best equipped of all pointing breeds for winter. Even short-hairs wear a virtual fur coat when compared to English pointers. I've yet to find Heidi unwilling to go out any time I've been game to face the elements.

Most negative comments on the versatile breeds come from bird hunting purists who just can't get used to stubby-tailed points. It is true that the continental dogs in general are much

Pheasant dogs need to be good retrievers. One of the best is Franz, a drahthaar owned by Miles Tratchel of Newton, Iowa.

less intense on point than are pointers and setters. In addition, they are perhaps a bit more inclined to chase critters with fur instead of concentrating on feathered game. But, after all, they were originally bred to hunt just about everything Europe has to offer, whether it runs or flies.

As a group, pointing dogs present some training difficulties that flushers do not. Their pointing instinct must be developed through contact with birds. They cannot be permitted to find and flush unless the hunter restricts them to gun range. If this is what the hunter wants, he or she should look to one of the flushing breeds. The advantage of pointing dogs over flushers, outside of the esthetics of shooting birds over point, is the ability to cover more ground without flushing all the birds out of range. The only way to gain this advantage is to have a dog that points reliably.

If you don't already own a hunting dog, what I've said to this point probably hasn't helped you choose between breeds, or even between pointing dogs and flushers. To do that, you have to think about where and how you hunt.

In my part of the country, more and more farm ground is going into the Conservation Reserve Program (CRP). This land is taken out of crop production for ten years and must be planted in some sort of cover. The result is more prime pheasant cover than we've seen in Iowa in years.

If you like to hunt this kind of wall to wall cover, consider the pointing breeds. The fact that they cover a lot more territory is only important if you have a lot of ground to be covered—and you certainly do in many of the big CRP fields.

If, on the other hand, you do most of your hunting along narrow waterways, small draws, or fence lines, the pointing breeds lose their advantage. If your typical cover is no wider than the range of your gun, then why not hunt with a dog that is a naturally close hunter? That's what the flushing breeds are meant to do.

In general, the flushers also work better in very heavy cover than do most pointing dogs. The thrill and appeal of a dog on point loses a lot when the cover is so thick that the dog is buried anyway.

Initially, hunters who haven't worked with dogs much are likely to be more comfortable with flushing dogs. They work in a relatively slow and thorough manner, much as should dogless hunters themselves. Those new to dogs are likely to be uncomfortable with the faster-moving pointing dogs, which will often be out of gun range. Also, the speed of these dogs may lead inexperienced hunters to believe that they are running by birds. Although this isn't often the case, it takes some convincing for those who aren't used to dogs.

The typical recommendation made to dogless hunters is to locate a pup out of the breed they have chosen, out of good hunting stock, and to train it. There are plenty of books which will help you to do this if you decide to go the puppy route. However, be prepared to discover that this training business isn't as simple as you might have been led to believe, especially in the case of pointing dogs. If training were such an easy thing, there would be a lot of starving professional dog trainers. Instead, trainers are pretty easy to find, and the better ones have all the business that they want.

Training does not require an enormous expenditure of time. In fact, a short training session daily is better than a couple of long sessions per week, when you're working with a pup. Like small children, pups have short attention spans.

Eventually, however, you have to work your bird dog on birds. Pigeons or training quail are the two leading choices. Now, in addition to being in the dog business, you are in the bird business. It isn't all that expensive, but it can pose a problem, particularly if you live in an urban area. Likewise, finding an area in which to work the dog on birds can pose a dilemma for the city dweller and may limit training to weekends.

What I am suggesting is that you may eventually determine that the services of a pro trainer—which may set you back $250 a month, more or less—are worth the cost if you're really interested in seeing your pup live up to its potential.

There is also another option. That is to acquire a mature dog instead of a pup. These come in two categories—started and broke.

The started dog is typically somewhere in the one- to two-year-old-age range. It will have been introduced to gunfire and birds. If it belongs to one of the pointing breeds, it should point well, although don't expect it to stand its birds forever. It probably will not retrieve to hand, although it may well go after downed birds. A started flushing dog should work within gun range, may chase rather than stopping to flush, and probably will retrieve fairly well. In either case, what should be left for you, the buyer, is to put on the finishing touches.

Depending on experience, age, breed, and the going market in your area, the average price for a started dog will be somewhere in the $500–$750 range. This is two or three times what you'd pay for a pup. However, the started dog is at least a year older than the pup. All those first-year vet bills have been paid. The big advantage, however, is that you can actually see—in fact, should demand to see—what the started dog can do on birds. With a pup, you're strictly buying potential.

I've had experience with both pups and started dogs. After Jake died and I needed another dog, I bought Heidi from a shooting preserve. She was fifteen months old. She pointed nicely, and although she didn't deliver to hand, she had good retrieving instincts and a very soft mouth.

I've found two drawbacks with Heidi. Initially, she was very shy around me and cowered a lot. She still acts the same way around people she doesn't know. I attribute this to the fact that she grew up in a kennel with a lot of other dogs and relatively limited human contact. It does not affect her performance on birds. In her first season on pheasants, she made nearly one hundred points and had fifty birds killed over her. She'd been given a lot of early work on woodcock because her kennel-mate, Rebel, nearly died of a kidney infection that fall. When you can finish the training process principally through hunting, it's a relatively painless way to develop a gun dog.

Heidi's other fault was chasing deer. I corrected that with an electronic collar, about which I'll have more to say later.

Rebel is my most recent puppy student. Being Jake's daughter, there was not much doubt about her potential. She is more of a "people" dog than was her sire, who also grew up in a kennel and tended to fit the "hunting machine" image of the pointer. She still relates much better to strangers than does Heidi, once again probably because she had a lot more human contact during puppyhood.

The price I paid for Rebel was right—she was the stud fee for a litter Jake sired. However, she eventually cost me about three hundred dollars in training fees. Even with all the work we put in together, she needed more contact with birds under a controlled situation, which she finally got when I left her at a shooting preserve for several weeks.

I also acquired Jake as a started dog, but he was several months older than Heidi. He had also had far more birds shot over him, and in fact almost fell into the broke dog category, even though he wasn't yet two. English pointers tend to develop quite quickly, and Jake knew just about all he had to about finding and pointing pheasants.

A fully broke dog, which should point or flush (depending upon the breed) and retrieve, all under control, is likely to set you back at least one thousand dollars. If you have the money to spend, or if you don't feel that you hunt enough to put the finishing touches on a started dog, or if you need a dog right now that will do it all, this is the way to go. My good friend Tom Huggler, who lost his fine setter Macbeth quite unexpectedly, had to go this route when he was faced with several months' worth of hunting and several thousand miles' worth of driving in an attempt to shoot every species of grouse in North America.

Whatever degree of training your dog possesses, you will almost certainly have some work to do before it becomes a reliable pheasant dog. The one trait a ringneck dog needs, which unfortunately is not innate like nose or desire, and which separates good pheasant dogs from four-legged disasters, is control.

Because pheasants run so much, they can make just about any dog blow its cool on some days. The good ones seldom lose their cool. The bad ones seldom keep it.

When a pheasant starts running, a flushing dog that takes after the bird full blast is almost certain to give you out-of-range flushes, unless you happen to be a track star. Likewise, the pointing dog that speeds after roosters may produce some points far beyond gun range, but not many shots. Dogs have to learn to work running birds in such a way that you can keep up. Whether you get a shot or not is uncertain, but you certainly won't if your dog breaks and runs every time pheasants start hotfooting it through the cover.

This is why it is absolutely imperative that a flushing dog stay in range at all times, probably no more than 30 yards from the gun, if that. I like to keep my pointing dogs within 75 yards, and if the birds are moving around a lot, I feel more comfortable if they are even closer. But when I get a point at 75 yards or so, I can often get there before the bird decides it's time to leave. Expecting your dogs to pin pheasants much farther out than that is being very optimistic. People who consistently get productive points at 200 yards either have much better dogs than I do or are hunting a different strain of pheasant.

Individual pointing dogs handle running birds in different ways. Theoretically, a pointing dog is supposed to remain in place until released. Pointer owners who expect this level of performance are the ones who say that pheasants ruin their dogs.

My dogs move when the bird moves. This may be bad manners in refined circles, but it tells me that I'm dealing with a runner. I can slow them down enough that, if the bird isn't determined to run over the horizon, I can probably get a flush in range.

Heidi's reaction on running birds is to give me almost a moving point. She'll tiptoe along, stopping if the bird stops, or if I whistle her or tell her to "whoa." Rebel's tactic is to lock up, wait, and perhaps glance over her shoulder to see if I'm coming. Then she'll dash another 20 or 30 yards and repeat the performance. What Reb does is harder on my nerves, because if she doesn't move off point, I never know until I've just about walked up to her whether the bird is there or not. It does, however, produce more solid points on runners that finally stop than does Heidi's

Control is critical in the development of a top-notch pheasant dog. Here Heidi, Larry Brown's shorthair, is getting a refresher course with the electronic collar.

semi-creeping performance. When she stops without being commanded to do so, Heidi almost certainly has the bird nailed. But in many cases, it will flush before she comes to a complete halt. In either case, the dogs have provided me ample warning that a bird is there, and most of the time they do it under decent control. Some days I have to work harder at it than others, especially when the birds are really running.

When I acquired Jake as an almost-broke dog, the one element he lacked was control. He had had hundreds of released pheasants and quail shot over him, and his points were things of beauty. However, running pheasants nearly ended our association.

Shortly after I got Jake, I was working him on a public hunting area before the season. The place had good cover and plenty of birds. Unfortunately, it was surrounded by private ground planted in corn, almost none of which had been harvested.

It was my luck to hit a day when the birds were running. Jake stopped when they did, and went after them when they ran. Eventually, the birds he was following ran off the area into a huge adjacent cornfield. I whistled and called and finally drove around the back roads looking for him until dark. No luck.

I left an old jacket near where I'd parked, hoping that he would return. But when I returned the next day, he was still nowhere to be found. I put up notices in nearby small town stores and cafes. All I could do was wait.

A couple of days later, I got a call from a farmer who had Jake. He thought the wiry pointer, a fairly uncommon breed in northern Iowa, was some sort of weird coon hound.

When I got Jake back, I knew that I had to establish control or get a different dog. That nose, one of the best I've ever seen at work, was attached to four of the best legs a dog could ever want. He'd point when the birds would hold or follow them forever in hopes that they would.

My solution was the electronic collar. It didn't take Jake long to understand that his boss now had a very long arm and that when he heard the whistle, he'd better respond, running bird or not.

I never lost Jake again. I won't say that I was ever totally comfortable with his range, but that is largely a matter of breeding. When I was really concerned with control, for example on a windy day when I figured we might have more trouble than normal with running birds, Jake wore the collar in the field. I will also use it occasionally while hunting Rebel, or much more rarely, on Heidi, if she seems to be getting a bit hardheaded.

There are a couple of myths about the electronic collar. One is that it is a cruel device. The second is that it should only be used by professionals.

Let's discuss the cruelty issue first. If a dog disobeys in the field, your alternatives without the collar are very limited. You can run the dog down and discipline it, which is often impossible to do. If you call the dog in and discipline it, how will it understand why it is being punished?

The electronic collar allows you to catch the dog in the act. As long as the dog has been trained to respond to a particular voice or whistle command, there is no cruelty whatsoever in using the collar if the dog disobeys. Use an electronic collar this way, and you will be doing exactly what the vast majority of pro trainers do, very few of whom do not use the device. On the other hand, if you use the electronic collar to take out your frustration on the dog, you may well ruin the dog—deservedly so.

I do not intend this to be a commercial for electronic collars. I believe in them, but they are not for all dogs. Neither are they for all dog owners.

I owned two pheasant dogs before I bought a collar. The first was Deke, a Brittany I acquired while working for the CIA in Morocco. Deke had had plenty of birds shot over him, mostly chukar and European quail. He was a reliable pointer and an excellent retriever.

That Moroccan experience transferred very well to woodcock and bobwhites. He handled both extremely well. However, running pheasants were another story. On a good day, he had maybe five minutes' worth of patience before he'd take off after them.

I think that the collar would have worked on Deke. I trained him on a check cord, and he knew that a long whistle blast meant to come. He simply chose to ignore it when he had a nose full of running ringneck. But he did well when the birds held and seldom lost a cripple. Thus, I'd rate him about average on pheasants.

When Deke died, I was anxious to have another dog. In September, I decided that I needed one for the coming season. My choice fell upon a started Irish setter named Nick. If you'd ever hunted with me and Nick, you would have assumed that his name was any of a number of other four-letter words. One of my hunting partners christened him "the red rocket."

Nick loved to hunt, had at least an average nose, some pointing instinct, and would chase cripples. He was also gun-shy. I didn't make him that way. The breeder from whom I bought him tried to establish control during Nick's puppy season by shooting him at long range when he flushed some birds rather than pointed. One of the pellets, I discovered a year or so later, was still lodged in Nick's foot.

Most pro trainers don't want to deal with gun-shy dogs. It is relatively easy to prevent but very hard to cure. With a lot of patience, graduating from .22 blanks at 100 feet to the .410 when a bird flushed, I managed to solve the problem. In the process, however, I lost what little control I ever had over Nick. I let him chase birds, especially when I shot, because I wanted him to associate hunting and guns with fun. After three frustrating seasons, I gave him away to a family looking for a pet. I doubt that the collar would have done much for him.

In the case of Nick and some other incorrigibles like him,

hunting dogless may be preferable. But for the most part, there is no substitute for a dog in pheasant cover. My advice to any serious pheasant hunter who doesn't have a dog is simple—get one.

I can only think of a couple of valid reasons for a pheasant hunter not owning a dog. Perhaps the hunter or someone in his or her family is severely allergic. Perhaps living circumstances do not allow housing a dog. Other than those excuses, I can't see why anyone who pursues the sport with dedication would choose to do so without a dog.

The expansion of the CRP makes canine assistance more critical. There are just more and more places where pheasants can go and where dogless hunters will get nothing but frustration.

Therefore, the most significant piece of advice I can offer to dogless hunters is to select the cover you hunt very carefully. Work narrow strips of cover, where it is almost impossible to walk by birds. Fencerows and narrow creeks are good bets, as are road ditches and railroad rights-of-way, where local laws permit.

Walk slowly. If the cover is much over a few feet wide, zigzag. Stop frequently. A surprisingly high percentage of your flushes will come when you pause for a few seconds.

But effectiveness in the field is not the sole reason, and perhaps not even the primary reason, why pheasant hunting should be done by a human-dog team. In our increasingly urban world, we spend most of our time working with other people or, more and more these days, with machines. Hunting remains one of the few pursuits in which we can participate with another species of animal. This human-dog relationship, which has existed for thousands of years, has a way of taking its human participants back in time, when it was really necessary to hunt for food in order to survive. I find this link with our own past to be an intriguing and refreshing aspect of the sport.

Apart, human and dog are inefficient hunters. A human can kill birds but because of weak senses has a poor chance of locating them. The dog can locate birds but without assistance stands a poor chance of killing them. Together, dog and human make a perfect hunting team.

When you, as the supposedly more intelligent member of this team, watch a dog unravel a pheasant's scent trail, using a sense of smell thousands of times keener than your own, you will feel almost as if you are watching a miracle unfold. Spend much time afield with a dog and you will soon learn why many experienced hunters say that they would rather hunt without a gun than without their dog.

Where to Hunt

T should be readily apparent that you have to hunt good cover in order to be a successful pheasant hunter. In my opinion, hunting in good cover ranks right up there with having a good dog and shooting well as key factors in bagging pheasants.

What is good pheasant cover? That depends on the topography of the region you hunt, the major crops in your area, the weather, and even the time of day.

Finding cover that holds pheasants isn't the only problem. Once you've found bird-holding cover, you have to be able to hunt it effectively. That depends not only on the cover itself but also on the composition of your hunting party. How many hunters do you have? Do they have any particular strengths or weaknesses as individuals or as a group which will make them more or less effective in particular cover types? How many dogs do you have? What kind of cover do they work best?

But let's begin at the beginning. You can't always select ideal cover, because you have to hunt what is available to you. Pheasant hunting in most areas requires gaining access to private land. Therefore, what is available to you depends on your ability to get permission to hunt from the landowner.

There are a few basic truths which hunters should keep in mind when asking permission, some of which I've touched on briefly elsewhere in this book.

Remember that if you're talking about opening day in a heavily hunted area, you need to make your arrangements well in advance. Remember also that permission tends to be easier to get as the season wears on and the number of hunters thins out. Finally, remember that landowners are more likely to give permission to one or two hunters they don't know than they are to an entire gang.

I doubt that I'd make much of an encyclopedia salesman, because I'm not very comfortable knocking on doors and asking permission. But I've gotten better at it over the years. For me, the direct approach seems to be the best.

I start by introducing myself and telling the landowners where I live. Then I'll ask them if the particular piece of ground I'm interested in hunting belongs to them. (Often, I'll be operating from a county plat book and will have a good idea of who owns what before I ask.) If they reply in the affirmative, I'll then ask them if they'd mind my hunting there.

A good 80–90 percent of the time, I'll get permission using this very simple and direct approach. When I do get turned down, the landowners—who are certainly well within their rights to say no—usually give me a good reason. There may be livestock in the field that I didn't spot, or they may have friends or relatives for whom they reserve hunting rights. If the latter is the case, the farmers will often invite me to return later in the season.

When I do get permission, I also ask the landowners where their property stops and the neighbors' starts. I avoid trespassing at all costs, and most landowners will have a higher opinion of responsible hunters who want to make sure they are hunting where they belong. A secondary advantage of this question is that it may reveal other parcels of land I haven't spotted which are also good bird cover.

Once I've found out where I can hunt, I then ask the landowners if their families enjoy pheasant dinners. Most farm families do, but very few farmers do much bird hunting. In that case, I tell the landowners that I'll be more than happy to share my good fortune with them.

I always make sure to follow through on this promise. Most of the time, I don't stop by immediately after the hunt to drop off a bird. Unless the landowners indicate that they are anxious to dress the birds themselves, I'm a firm believer in sharing cleaned game with my hosts. I'd rather take the birds home, clean them thoroughly and properly, and drop off a couple of frozen roosters on my next trip.

I prefer doing it this way for a couple of reasons. First, I may have collected birds which are badly shot up. I save those for myself and use less damaged ones to give to landowners. Also,

waiting gives you an excuse for a return trip. There are few landowners, especially if they have given you permission once already, who will turn you down if you show up on their doorstep
with a couple of birds in hand.

I continue to be amazed at the number of places I hunt with
excellent cover and good bird numbers where no one has ever
offered to share their bag with the landowner. In a normal season, I give away far more pheasants than I eat myself. On at least
three occasions one season, I made deliveries of two or three
birds at a time to one particularly large farm family, whose property happened to play host to a particularly large number of
pheasants.

This simple and inexpensive way of saying thank you has
cemented a number of continuing relationships with landowners. Other hunters I know make different kinds of gifts to
farmers. A Wisconsin friend of mine always brings along a selection of his state's fine cheeses. Other friends have given landowners a bottle of good scotch, which works fine as long as you're
not dealing with a teetotaler.

The important thing is to thank the landowner sincerely, and
I feel that something tangible reinforces my gratitude. Sharing
your game with a farmer seems especially appropriate. After all,
who provides the food and shelter that those pheasants enjoy?

When you are hunting a new area, one of the best ways to
find good cover is through a local contact. One word of warning
here: the local contact should also be a pheasant hunter. He or
she will not only have access to private ground, but most likely it
will be good pheasant cover. Nonhunting contacts may be able to
introduce you to farmer friends of theirs and think that they are
doing you a big favor when the only cover available to hunt is a
couple of blades of grass in the middle of a bare pasture.

Ed Wilson, my niece's husband, frequently swaps hunts with
me. There's nothing formal about our arrangement. I hunt with
him on his covers in northern Iowa, and then he comes and
hunts in central Iowa with me. I've done the same thing with a
number of other dedicated pheasant hunters that I've met over
the years.

A variation of this is to swap hunts for different types of
game. If I have someone who has shown me a lot of good
pheasant hunting, and if they seem to have an interest in something more exotic, at least from an Iowa hunter's standpoint,
then I'll take them after grouse and woodcock. I can't show my
friend Dave Prine much better pheasant shooting than he has

within 15 miles of where he lives, but I did take him along on a northern Michigan grouse and woodcock hunt. Good local contacts often turn into good hunting companions, people with whom you want to share more time afield.

But in many cases, you have to find the cover yourself. One way to spot good cover is by looking for the pheasant's preferred food supply. In my part of the country, pheasants relate very closely to corn. It not only comprises much of their diet during the hunting season, it also provides excellent cover for the birds until it has been harvested. Even after the harvest, hunting corn can be quite productive.

I started this book with a discussion of a classic drive and block operation in standing corn. You don't see those maneuvers much any more, and I for one don't shed tears over their disappearance.

When I look at standing corn, I have about the same reaction as Indiana Jones faced with a room full of snakes. I hate standing corn! It encourages birds to run and dogs to run after them. Getting good shots in the midst of a forest of 7-foot stalks is also tough.

I avoid standing corn when at all possible. A very late harvest for the 1986 opener resulted in my partner and I getting skunked for the entire opening weekend. I fired one shot during those two days. That "chance" came about half an hour before closing time on Sunday on a bird at the extreme limit of effective range. I shot more out of frustration than from any real hope of bagging a bird.

That weekend, there was corn everywhere. We hunted adjacent fields of grass and weeds, but the corn was where the pheasants were. We also tried working the corn itself, but the fields were so big that it would have taken a reinforced platoon of drivers and blockers to cover them.

I'm very happy to say that there hasn't been a late harvest since then.

Once the harvest began in earnest that year, I started to have some luck. The CRP was just beginning then, and very few fields had been taken out of crop production. That meant that the birds were being pushed into cover along the edges of the picked fields, because that was mostly all they had left. Waterways, fence lines, and ditches began to produce birds.

Even though the hunting did pick up as the season went on and the corn came down, it never got as good as I had hoped it would. A tough opener, particularly when it is a result of a lot of standing crops, can mean that there will be plenty of birds around for the dedicated late season pheasant hunters, those who continue to pursue ringnecks long after opening day. In 1986, that was not the case.

I bagged a total of thirty-six roosters that year, averaging a bit over three hours per bird. While I wasn't dissatisfied, given the bird population, both the total and the average time per bird bagged do not compare favorably with years when bird numbers have been up. Cover plays a critical role in that equation, as we shall see shortly.

Twenty of those thirty-six birds bagged came from within gunshot of a waterway, creek, or river. That kind of cover is more or less a permanent fixture here in Iowa. Although small waterways do get bulldozed and tiled away, these changes are much less frequent than the annual rotation of crops in a given field. In short, waterways tend to be very reliable cover areas, and I focus on them when other types of good cover are in short supply.

Nineteen eighty-nine was a significant contrast to 1986. My total bag was sixty-three roosters, hunting almost exactly the same amount of time as in 1986. This averaged out to well under two hours per bird.

The difference was cover—both the cover in which the birds could nest and the cover in which I did most of my hunting.

By 1989 the CRP was well established in Iowa. Nineteen eighty-eight was atypical because, due to the severe drought, many of the CRP fields were mowed to provide fodder for livestock. These fields grew back to excellent cover the following year, in some cases even better than they had been before being mowed.

Nesting cover and winter cover are two factors which have a significant impact on pheasant populations. Not having had a severe winter since 1985, Iowa has had no real problems with winter cover in recent years. But nesting cover has been a limiting factor, ever since much of the state switched to intensive row-crop farming.

The CRP has largely solved this problem throughout much of the pheasant's range. Where we had little nesting cover in the spring of 1986, there were thousands of acres of it in 1989. The result was a dramatic surge in pheasant numbers.

The CRP has also changed my focus as a hunter. Although I still took nineteen roosters along waterways in 1989, the majority of my birds—thirty-five in all—came from CRP acres. These areas are thus of double benefit to the pheasant hunter: not only do they provide plenty of nesting and winter cover, but excellent hunting cover as well.

The CRP fields I hunt are large blocks of cover, at least 40 acres, often much larger than that. The CRP requires farmers to plant set-aside fields in trees or some sort of perennial grass. In Iowa, the choice is almost always grass, usually one or more of the prairie grass varieties. All prairie grass, especially when it has had a year or two to get established, is excellent pheasant cover. It is tall enough and thick enough to hide the birds, yet not so dense that they can't run in it. I find these huge fields of grass a delight to hunt. While it is not easy walking, I prefer it by far to slogging through a marsh, not to mention slinking between rows of standing corn.

Hunters used to working narrower, less imposing chunks of cover may be intimidated by CRP fields. But unlike enormous blocks of standing corn, CRP ground does not require an army of hunters. Although in some cases, especially late in the season, several hunters may be more effective, a lone hunter with a good dog can do very well in this kind of cover.

Initially, one's reaction is that the birds can be anywhere in cover like that. While pheasants do have lots of options in many of these fields, I often find that they prefer certain specific areas within what at first appears to be a relatively featureless ocean of cover. If you hunt most set-aside fields three or four times, I think that you also will find this to be true. You will discover that the birds relate to some very subtle variations in the cover—perhaps a change from one type of grass to another, perhaps an old ditch or fence line, perhaps a slight change in elevation.

But even keying in on these preferred "mini-habitats," you are not likely to find many birds without canine assistance. Except perhaps on opening day, if you happen to hit one of the smaller CRP fields with lots of birds and if you have lots of hunters, your chances of successfully hunting this kind of cover dogless are minimal.

How do you tell a good CRP field from a bad one, if indeed there is such a thing? Although the majority of this kind of cover in good pheasant country will hold birds, some set-aside fields are much better bets than others.

Assuming two CRP fields with equal inherent potential for offering refuge to birds—that is to say, the same quality of tall, dense grass cover—the difference will usually be what is found in adjacent fields.

One grass field surrounded by a number of other grass fields is not likely to act as much of a bird magnet. Likewise, such a field surrounded by shortgrass pasture or woodlands but with no crops anywhere in the vicinity does not have a lot of potential. Both of these situations occur quite regularly in southern Iowa, where large livestock operations are common. There can be such a thing as taking too many fields out of row-crop production, and that seems to be the case in parts of Iowa's traditionally top pheasant region.

Find a big block of set-aside ground—I prefer at least 80 acres—with little other good bird-holding cover but plenty of crops in the vicinity, and in all likelihood you've found the ringneck version of treasure island. Once again, as mentioned earlier, you need to keep your eye out for a food supply. In this case, the birds are not living right in their kitchen, as they do in standing corn, but they do prefer staying within easy strolling distance of their pantry.

Let me illustrate by following the cover changes on, and surrounding, one particular area that I've hunted for several years.

This particular piece of cover consists of two farms and totals about 600 acres. It is an entire section minus a corner which is cut off where a road jogs. In other words, I can hunt everything within the boundaries formed by the gravel roads on each of the four sides.

Its "permanent" cover consists of an excellent creek, running a full mile from the north to the south end of the section. The creek is joined by a little tributary about halfway down, forming another strip of cover half a mile long.

I first hunted the ground in 1985, late in the season, and shot a couple of birds which were taking refuge from the cold and deep snow in the dense creek bank cover.

In 1986 most of the ground adjacent to the creek was planted to corn. As soon as the corn was picked, the farmer turned his cattle into the field. I made one hunt on the place, and by the time I got there, the cattle had stomped the cover flat.

In 1987 the smaller of the two farms on the section—160 acres—went into the CRP. I made eight trips to the area, hunting a total of twenty hours, and bagged twelve birds.

The surrounding cover, in the fields just across the adjacent roads, was almost perfect. There was picked corn to the north, picked grain and pasture to the east and west, pasture and a grass field to the south. Eventually, toward the end of the season, the birds began to flush wild and fly into the grass south of the road, where I couldn't hunt. It was just about the only nearby escape cover available.

In 1988 the grass on the smaller farm was all mowed, making it virtually worthless as cover. However, about 80 acres of the larger farm went into the CRP. Hunting this cover and the creek, I took four roosters in a total of six and a half hours.

In 1989, the cover on the small farm had grown back even thicker than it had been two seasons previously. In addition, all of the large farm except about 100 acres was in set-aside. The surrounding cover was exactly like it had been in 1987, except that the grass field to the south was mowed for hay.

I hunted pheasants on this area eleven times for a total of twenty-three hours and put sixteen roosters in the bag. I also knocked down two others and lost them in the heavy cover.

Does that sound to you like I was overworking an area? Well, have you ever tried hunting 500 acres of solid cover? On the majority of my trips, I was hunting alone. I could have spent all day there and not hunted everything.

That season, with a large and well-established block of fantastic habitat and no surrounding escape cover, the birds were reluctant to leave the area. They would simply fly some distance and then settle back into the cover. The only exception to this pattern was when they were pushed up against one of the boundary roads, when they would reluctantly leave their sanctuary. On several occasions, heading for home just after shooting hours closed, I would spot numerous birds walking or flying back into the cover.

The hunting on that particular section held up very well, from the first time I hunted it in early November to my last trip in early January.

When I say that the hunting remained good, that is obviously a relative statement. Although the hunting got progressively tougher, the place never got shot out.

On my first few trips, about all I had to do was follow whichever dog I happened to be using. Rebel, who is better suited to that kind of cover than Heidi, produced one limit for me in half an hour.

On those earlier hunts, the birds did not seem to run much when pressured. The main problem was that just in the normal course of moving around, they left a lot of scent to be sorted out. But once the dogs really got on something hot, it wasn't long before I had a bird in the air, usually over a point.

Even on an enormous area such as this one with a high bird

population, you can't have it easy forever. Eventually, the birds
began to react to pressure and to the experience they've gained
through repeated contacts with hunters, dogs, and guns.

Hunting that one area repeatedly in that same season taught
me a lot about pheasant behavior. The birds, when exposed to
enough pressure, will run more in heavy cover than I had previously believed. On numerous occasions, I watched both of my
dogs working hot scent for at least fifteen minutes and coming up
empty. The pheasants became clever enough to zigzag around in
the cover, apparently having learned through conditioning that
this was the way to thwart a dog.

On my earlier hunts, I could not have predicted where my
shots might come. A bird might just as easily present a chance in
the middle of the section as along one of the roads—perhaps even
more so. By the end of the season, nearly all my shots were coming when I managed to push a bird into a corner and it would be
forced to fly. These were all on edges of one sort or another.

In late December, I hunted that area with Chuck Gates and
his son Josh. With three of us, plus two shorthairs, we were able
to cut down on the number of birds that could run around us.

My first chance came just south of an abandoned farmstead,
where the rooster had skulked through the grass to within gunshot of the open farmyard. Josh took a bird off the northwest
corner, where a number of birds had escaped on previous hunts
by flying directly over a feedlot and house just across the road.
But this bird went north instead of west, and Josh took advantage of the clear shot. We turned east, paralleling the north fence,
and Chuck took another bird a quarter of a mile down right out of
the road ditch.

Josh bagged the next bird, a cripple which we recovered after
a long chase, off a fence running south between two set-aside
fields. Although this wasn't classic edge cover, that subtle cover
break provided by the fence had paid off for me on previous
hunts as well.

Another rooster came out from along the creek, just parallel
to the fence where Josh had made his shot. With both dogs on
point, Chuck had ample warning.

The last bird of the day got himself trapped in the corner of a
set-aside field, where it butted up against a frozen pond surrounded by open pasture. It hit the ice and bounced several times
when Chuck dropped it.

Yes, birds will run in that kind of cover. But if just following
the dog ceases to work, try hunting in such a way that the bird's

options become very limited. It worked for me on that hunt, as well as on other late-season visits to that same section. Two of the last three birds I killed there waited until the dog and I had pushed them right up to the road. They were nice shots over points and easy retrieves right off the gravel.

I don't think my late season experience on that set-aside ground was atypical. Although I haven't hunted that kind of cover extensively, simply because it hasn't existed in my part of the country until recently, other areas also produced similar results that year.

Jim Schlender, an editor friend of mine who is originally from Wisconsin but currently resides in Georgia, came back to the Midwest to hunt pheasants with me in 1989. Teaming up with my partners, Chuck and Josh Gates, the four of us accounted for half a dozen birds from a somewhat smaller CRP area. It was December, well over a month after the season opened, there was a 40 MPH wind blowing, and given those circumstances, I was amazed that we did so well. In addition, we lost two birds, undoubtedly with the heavy cover and strong wind being major contributing factors.

But more unusual than the number of birds we dropped was the number of birds we flushed, the vast majority out of range. Even admitting that we had some reflushes, we conservatively estimated that the 200 acres or so we hunted must have held well over one hundred birds.

The next day, weather conditions improved considerably. Although the thermometer hovered just above the single digits, the wind had died almost entirely. Only a couple of inches of new snow could have made for a better setting for a December hunt. It was the final day of Jim's Iowa hunt, and I was hoping to show him a repeat of the previous day's action.

We teamed up with Miles Tratchel, a hunting partner of mine from Jasper County. Miles, like so many of the dedicated pheasant hunters I know, hunts behind an excellent dog, a drahthaar named Franz who is one of the best cripple-finders I have seen. Miles happens to be a confirmed side-by-side shooter, haunting the pheasant fields with his SKB Model 100 20 gauge.

We started the hunt by working down a wide, brushy fence line, and then swinging into a draw that petered out in the middle of an open field. About halfway up the draw, Jim made a nice shot on the only rooster we saw for the first hour or so of the hunt.

Jim's second chance came on a rooster that gave him a nice

crossing shot. He was behind with his first try, and his malfunctioning pump kept him from firing a second time.

The three of us took a break just across the fence into a large set-aside field, while Jim cleared up his mechanical problems. Franz, who is extremely well trained, sat patiently at Miles's feet. Heidi is not nearly that obedient but has little tendency to wander off. However, when we were set to go again, she was nowhere in sight.

I blew my whistle but got no response. I hang bells on my pheasant dogs, something I've picked up from grouse hunters. On that cold, quiet morning, I would have heard her had she been moving anywhere within 200 yards of me.

We were just below a gentle rise in the ground. Walking to the top, we spotted her on point. I moved in and a rooster flushed about 10 feet in front of her nose, giving me an easy shot.

I'd no more than picked that bird up when Franz nailed another one, just off to Miles's right side. He tried to get Jim in position for a shot, but the rooster didn't wait around. Miles dropped it hard with his first barrel.

The three of us spread out in the thigh-high grass, Heidi and I within gunshot of a fence which separated our field from picked corn, Jim next to me, and Miles and Franz off to my far right.

Both dogs were making game. While Heidi stuck fairly close to the fence, Franz angled farther out into the cover. Jim and Miles followed him.

As we topped another rise, a dozen or so birds flushed about 150 yards ahead. Before they had settled back into the cover, another bunch took wing, and another, and another. We all stood there transfixed, men and dogs. Heidi was right by my side, and it was almost as if she were on point. But her head swiveled slowly from side to side, as she tracked those bunches of departing birds.

If those two Poweshiek County fields I described earlier were a pheasant hunter's Garden of Eden, this Jasper County cover had to be heaven. After the hunt, when Jim and I compared impressions, we decided that during the departure of those several squadrons of pheasants, we saw easily twice as many birds as we had the day before.

Once the shock wore off, we started hunting again. We'd still move an occasional group of ten or twelve birds, always out of range, but the mass flush seemed to be over.

Heidi and I were working toward a creek which formed one boundary of the cover. She got birdier and birdier as we de-

scended in the direction of the wooded stream. Finally, she settled into another hard point. The bird flushed back in the direction of my partners, who had turned out into the cover a couple of
hundred yards away. The only problem I had was waiting until
they weren't in the line of fire. I added number two to my game
pouch.

Meanwhile, the sound of an occasional shot told me that
Franz was pinning some of the scattered birds for Miles and Jim
also. But I was too busy watching Heidi to worry much about
them. She spun in her tracks, freezing for the third time.

I've never killed three birds with three shots, all over points,
and that thought may have been running through my mind as I
moved in on the dog. I resolved to take my time, and that was my
undoing. Instead of shooting when it felt right, I let the close-
flushing rooster get out a ways farther. What should have been
an easy chance resulted in a bird with both legs dropped, and my
second barrel failed to connect.

The bird cleared a rise, going back the way we came, with me
and Heidi in hot pursuit. Unfortunately, by the time we reached
the top of the hill, the bird was out of sight. It was only a couple of
hundred yards to the fence where the field ended against picked
corn. We worked it as well as possible, and although I'm quite
sure the cripple came down somewhere in the vicinity, Heidi
couldn't come up with him. A couple of times, when she pointed
along the bank of the creek, I thought we had him. Instead, two
hens flushed. There was so much scent and so much cover that I
could only fault my own poor shooting and not the dog work.

We reversed course. Bird number three came out about a
quarter mile down the creek but didn't wait around for Heidi to
point. I didn't wait on this bird either, and he finished my limit.

I had a couple of other looks at roosters at the fringe of range
as we worked to catch up with my partners. I spotted them
across a frozen creek, working a tiny patch of weedy corn right in
the angle of the fences that formed the boundary of our field.

I heard another shot as I scrambled up the steep bank, where
I found Heidi on point. "Need another bird?" I yelled to them,
now within easy hailing distance. "We've got our six!" replied
Miles. I walked past Heidi and kicked up another rooster.

Checking my watch, I found that we'd been hunting for
about two and a half hours. Taking a three-man limit that
quickly, and seeing the numbers of birds we did, is pretty unusual in the middle of the season.

"I didn't know Iowa pheasant hunting was like this," said

Jim with a huge smile on his face. "I thought yesterday was good."

"So did I," I replied. "I think Miles has been holding out on me."

"I don't recall ever seeing anything like this so late in the season," confirmed Miles.

Because of their size and capacity to offer good winter shelter to the birds, big CRP fields have definitely become my favorite spots for late-season hunts. But they are not the only places where you can catch up with winter birds.

When I reviewed my 1989 notes, I was not surprised to find that I'd killed more birds in set-aside ground than anywhere else. What did surprise me was that in the entire season I didn't kill a single bird in picked corn.

My feelings about picked corn are significantly different from my abhorrence of standing corn. About the only thing I have against it is the fact that the cover is not as conducive to solid points as are grass fields or streams with weedy banks. I didn't bag any birds in corn in 1989 mainly because I didn't spend much time hunting it. There were too many other good places to work, and because the harvest was so early, many of the fields were fall-plowed before the end of November.

An afternoon hunt in mid-December back in 1986 is a good example of the fact that picked corn can be very good, even late in the season.

Dave Prine and I started by working a couple of creeks and draws, and we were seeing plenty of birds. Unfortunately, they were all wild. It looked like one of those days when the roosters were wearing their Nikes and you need an antiaircraft gun to reach them.

Then we hit a field where his uncle had been combining not more than a couple of days earlier. We were hunting behind Dave's Labs, simply working up the rows one way, turning around at the fence and moving over a few rows, and hunting back the other way.

Dave already had a couple of birds in the bag, and my first shot came on a chance that made me stretch the old Sauer's modified tube for all it was worth. His black Lab, Luke, returned me a big old bird with a tail over 2 feet long.

My next two birds came out literally right at my feet, and had I been working Rebel, I'm sure I would have enjoyed the advance warning of a point. But both shots were easy ones, and I had one of those memorable three-for-three days. So did Dave. In fact, I

usually shoot better when I hunt with him. I think it has something to do with the fact that he's such a good shot and I'm trying
to avoid embarrassing myself.

There were at least three good reasons that explain our
success on that hunt. The first is that the field was recently
picked, and it's possible that the birds, used to the safety afforded
by the standing corn, simply moved back in once the combine
left.

The second is that a cold front was moving in. It was sunny
when we started our hunt. By the time we finished, the wind had
switched around to the north, it had started spitting snow, and
the temperature had dropped about ten degrees. Birds that sense
approaching fronts will often gorge themselves in anticipation of
a storm. These pheasants all had bulging crops.

The third reason is that the field was very weedy. All cornfields are not equal. The better ones, whether you should be so
foolish as to prefer to hunt them standing or take the more sensi-
ble approach and wait until they are picked, are those that have
cover other than the corn itself. Foxtail, an obnoxious weed
which is often the subject of winter TV commercials for herbicide
here in Iowa, is frequently the culprit in this part of the country.
Dave's uncle's herbicide hadn't worked, leaving lots of foxtail
and plenty of places for pheasants to hide, even after the field was
picked.

Finally, the birds didn't have all that many options. There
was little set-aside ground that season. And from the actions of
the birds we found along brushy creeks and in draws, it was
obvious that those areas had been hunted pretty hard.

Now that the CRP is well established, I would not expect to
have such good luck on a late-season hunt in picked corn, unless
I just happened to be fortunate enough to catch the birds out
feeding. Earlier in the year, on the other hand, picked corn is
often quite productive.

To my way of thinking, the old wisdom about trying to in-
terpret a pheasant's daily schedule is not a good way to select
cover. If you watch pheasants before the season, you will see that
they are indeed birds of habit, moving out to feed at about the
same time every day, unless severe weather interrupts this pattern. However, pressure from hunters causes them to adapt very
quickly. They feed when they can, and they spend the rest of
their time trying to keep away from these strange and relatively
efficient two-legged predators.

My major concern is to select cover, within the scope of what is available to me, that best suits the group—both human and canine—with which I'm hunting. If I'm by myself and have both dogs along, I can tackle about anything. I'll usually run Rebel, who covers lots of territory, in big grass fields. On narrow creeks or places where the cover is very dense, such as marshes, Heidi will get the nod.

Just as there are differences between set-aside fields, there are also differences between those long, narrow areas often referred to as strip cover. I divide strip cover into a number of subcategories. Where I hunt, the major ones are waterways, ditches, fence lines, and railraods.

Of these subcategories, you have probably already detected that waterways are my favorite. Fence lines are often too narrow and conducive to running, while road ditches force you to deal with passing traffic and the proximity of houses. Railroads can be excellent, and there was a time when I used to hunt them a lot. Perhaps the only reason I don't hunt them as much anymore is because I have access to more good CRP and waterway cover on private ground.

When it comes to waterways, I prefer a stream which falls into the creek or small river category, something not too wide. My dogs aren't trained to take hand signals, and if I drop a bird they don't spot on the far bank, I may have to go after it myself. In those cases, I prefer something narrow enough to jump, or at least shallow enough to wade across without getting too wet.

Most of the streams I hunt have no more than 20 yards or so of cover on either bank. The cover is largely of the knee-to-waist-high grass and weed variety, with a few trees thrown in here and there. If the stream runs through or near picked corn or soybeans, I'm fairly confident that birds will use its banks for cover.

A steep slope with several feet of drop to the waterline and with cover growing all the way down the banks affords good winter cover for late-season birds. But even when hunting these areas earlier in the year, it is a good idea to encourage your dog to drop over the edge to check things out from time to time. If there is a relatively wide strip of cover above the bank, one has a tendency to work that out and ignore what lies over the edge.

On a hunt in western Iowa, Jim Cole and I were working a fence line right along a small creek that dropped off quite abruptly. In one spot where the bank had eroded almost to the point of collapsing the fence, Heidi stuck her head through the wire and pointed.

I walked over behind her and looked down the weed-covered

Waterways with good, weedy cover on the banks are excellent spots to hunt for pheasants.

bank. I motioned Jim over to join me.

"No way can I get down to flush the bird," I said. "Get ready and I'll kick some dirt over the edge." I sent a few clods rolling down the bank, bringing the rooster cackling out of his hiding place.

The clever bird stayed below the top of the bank when he flushed, and although Jim and I both rocked him with our first barrels, it took my second shot to finish him off.

"I'll bet you anything that's an old rooster," I told Jim. His long black spurs and streaming tailfeathers proved me right when Heidi brought him back.

The English River in Poweshiek County is undoubtedly one of the more productive streams I have hunted. It is also fairly difficult for a lone hunter, even with a dog. A small stream which hardly deserves the title of river in the stretches I've hunted, the English has steep banks that in most places drop a good 20 feet from the fields above.

I was driving down a county road, looking for new places to hunt, the first time I worked the English. I sat in the truck on the bridge, looking along its weed-choked banks. It ran straight away from the road for about half a mile along the section that interested me. I was lucky enough to get permission, and with a prevailing south wind, Heidi and I started our hunt on the north bank.

The problem, I soon discovered, was that most of the good cover was below the top of the bank. The farmer had left only a narrow strip adjacent to the field. Much of that, however, was choked with heavy brush and small trees. I convinced Heidi to drop over the edge and work the bank. The cover was too thick for me to work right above her on the edge, so I stayed just outside, along the edge of the field, out of sight of the dog. I listened carefully for any change in the music of her bell.

A whitetail bounded up the bank on my side and out across the field, about 50 yards in front of me. That temporary distraction caused me to lose track of Heidi, and the next thing I knew, I couldn't hear her bell anymore.

Picking a break in the cover, I shoved my way through to the edge. The bank was in shadow, and had it not been for the white tip of her tail and her blaze orange collar, I doubt that I would have been able to spot her dark form on point.

"Come on, Heidi," I said. "That's just where the deer was bedded down."

I'd just turned my back when I heard the distinctive sound of pheasant wings. I turned around and took a snap shot at a bird making his exit down the stream. Under the best of circumstances, I'm not that good when I'm shooting down on birds, and this was not the best of circumstances.

We hit the line fence without any more action and walked picked corn back out to the road. Disappointed but undaunted, I decided the south bank was still worth the effort. We worked the road ditch down to the landowner's south line fence, a couple of hundred yards beyond the river. My plan was to follow that to the end of the field, then work north back to the river, and back out along the bank.

Neither fence produced any birds. However, the south bank was another story. Except in a couple of spots, it was open enough that I could walk on top and look down on what the dog was doing. That was the only way I was able to drop the first bird, which didn't wait for Heidi to point. He bounced in the picked corn on my side, above the bank.

Although the pheasant is largely a private land bird throughout much of its range, the bird can be hunted successfully in public areas.

Bird number two came over a nice point. This one flushed while I was debating chucking corncobs or clambering down the bank. He was also an easy retrieve.

Just as I approached a thick patch of thornbushes, which were going to cause me to detour into the field and out of sight of Heidi, she got very birdy. The rooster broke cover, and I dropped him through the branches on the second shot, thankful for what grouse hunting had taught me.

This bird dropped smack in the middle of the English. Heidi, in her first season of hunting with me, had never made a water retrieve. I was therefore very happy when she waded out into the stream and picked up the soggy bird. Unfortunately, my happiness was premature. She immediately decided that she did not like the taste of wet feathers and put the bird down right where she'd found him. No amount of coaxing or scolding could make her change her mind. I finally slithered down the bank and waded out myself, lucky that the temperature was only in the forties and the water only calf deep.

One of the secondary advantages of hunting creekbank cover is that you can often pin the birds between you and the stream. Although I've heard that pheasants can swim, I have never seen it. What I have observed through long experience is that when faced with a stream more than a good jump wide a pheasant will often hold very tight.

One problem my dogs and I had in 1988, the driest year I've ever hunted, was that this strategy didn't work in most places. Streams which were normally too wide to jump and too deep to wade didn't even have muddy bottoms.

Opening day should have tipped me off on things to come. Working what was usually a 20-foot-wide, waist-deep creek, Heidi was clearly on a runner. When she locked on at the top of the bank, I felt I had him. I knew that there was virtually no cover on the other side.

Heidi seemed almost as stunned as I when I walked by her and didn't flush anything. Then she took off down the creek bed in hot pursuit, raising dust as her feet hit the dirt. The bird turned out to be a youngster, and had he not been, I'm sure she wouldn't have pointed him where he tried to sit it out in a little clump of weeds on the far bank.

That year, it wasn't long before the birds figured out that dry streams were perfect places to get down and run like hell.

I've already explained, in an earlier chapter, how public areas are often much more productive than the average hunter would expect. They often consist of large blocks of very heavy cover, and like the set-aside fields, they can hold surprisingly good numbers of birds. The major problem is that some of them, usually those near large population centers, receive quite a bit of hunting pressure.

I've had some of my best luck hunting public areas which were established with waterfowl in mind. Other hard-core pheasant hunters I know have had the same experience. Steve

Grooms, in particular, has a strange love affair with swamp-dwelling roosters, and while there are places I'd really rather do my hunting, I have had good results working marshes, especially toward the tail end of the season.

In fact, my final birds of the season in 1978, 1980, 1981, 1983, and 1988 all came from public marshes. When you consider how much more time I spend on private land as opposed to public, you can see the value of these areas for late-season birds.

Duck marshes don't get a lot of pressure early, for the simple reason that pheasant hunters figure—probably correctly—that all the shooting and activity from the waterfowlers won't make for a good situation, either for them or the birds. But the duck season closes at least a month before pheasant season. By then, most pheasant hunters have given up, and those who do work the marshes don't have a lot of competition.

Public areas, like big set-aside fields, require a good dog. If anything, the cover on many public areas, and certainly on marshes, is going to be denser than what you are likely to encounter on most private land. Marsh ground is no prize to walk before it freezes, and even after ice-up, with all its hummocks, it offers much trickier footing than more traditional upland cover. It will wear you out in a hurry if you're not in shape, especially when it's cold and you are wrapped in several layers of clothing. But that is one reason why marshes are such good late-season cover. The birds are often way back off the beaten path, where many hunters lack either the capacity or the desire to go.

Although my pointers—especially Heidi, who goes through heavy cover like a bulldozer—can hunt this cover relatively well, it is really better suited to flush dogs. Marshes are great places for Labs, whether you happen to be hunting ducks or pheasants.

As I mentioned in the last chapter, strip cover is also better hunted with flush dogs or with a relatively slow and methodical pointing dog. I have to do a lot of hacking with Reb in narrow cover, as I did with Jake.

Perhaps a good way to end this chapter is by referring to the Pheasants Forever slogan, "Think Habitat." Habitat, or lack thereof, will make or break a bird population. Choosing the proper hunting habitat and matching it to the capabilities of you, your hunting party, and your dogs will ensure the success of your hunt.

Tactics

came very close to omitting this chapter. I am a bit of a heretic on the subject of tactics, as I am on the importance of weather to the pheasant hunter. Both, in my opinion, are overemphasized.

Considering the fact that I've discussed the use of various tactical maneuvers in preceding chapters, you may now think it a bit odd that I should downplay the importance of the subject. Most of the tactics I have discussed—driving standing corn and sneaking roadside ringnecks, in particular—are maneuvers that I seldom use these days. My notebooks convince me that I bag at least 90 percent of my birds simply by turning one of my dogs loose in good cover and letting her do her thing. If you have a good pair of legs, a good dog, and good cover to hunt, you will put birds in the bag without having to resort to much in the way of clever maneuvers.

Much of what passes for "pheasant hunting tactics" is, in my opinion, nothing more than simple common sense. You don't need a background in military science, or in animal behavior, to hunt pheasants successfully. I am convinced that hunters who devise elaborate schemes to corner pheasants would probably bag more birds if they spent less time scheming and more time walking.

Nevertheless, there are instances where a bit of advance planning can increase a hunter's odds of getting a good shot at a rooster. Before we take a look at some of those situations, we need to consider what these "tactics" are designed to accomplish.

Although all pheasant hunters need to master the block and drive maneuver, often the best tactic is simply following a good dog in good cover.

You don't read much about tactics for hunting grouse, woodcock, or quail. In the case of grouse and woodcock, once you've located the birds, the major problem is being able to take a shot when you get a flush. Even when the birds are pointed, the cover is often so thick that you either can't see the departing bird or you and your gun are so tangled in the cover that you can't shoot. If you have a partner, you might be able to arrange it so that one of you is in the clear. With those forest-dwelling birds, there just isn't much more tactical planning to be done.

Quail hunting may be even less tactical. In its classic form, it simply boils down to turning the dogs loose and following them. Once a covey is pointed, you can try maneuvering for good shots, as with grouse and woodcock. However, quail are usually out in the open, at least when compared with woodcock, and don't present quite the same difficulties. Trying to get between quail and the nearest cover is a tactic which is sometimes employed, almost always unsuccessfully. Your presence on a bobwhite's chosen flight path will do little to discourage the bird, and little brown bombs buzzing past your head are much harder to hit than when they are flying away from you.

Whoever invented pheasant tactics—probably an outdoor writer trying to sell a story with a new twist—recognized a basic difference between pheasants and the birds mentioned above. When it comes to the desired means of escape, a pheasant would rather use its legs than its wings.

The ringneck's propensity to run lies at the heart of just about every tactic I'm aware of. The problem, however, is that the birds can also fly. And in most kinds of cover, they can simply hide and not do either.

Driving standing corn, quite thoroughly described in chapter 1, was almost certainly the first maneuver to come into widespread use in pheasant hunting. Just to review, very briefly, the successful recipe for one of these operations includes the right amount of standing corn, the right number of hunters (smart enough not to shoot one another) to cover the field, and a goodly number of relatively uneducated pheasants inhabiting the field. Dogs are not a requirement and in fact should not participate unless they are under the *total* control of their handler. The object is to make the birds run, but not too far too fast. If this happens, they might scoot out the sides of the field beyond the range of the drivers before they reach the blockers.

The pheasants should be of the relatively uneducated variety for the same reason. Battle-scarred veterans are likely to beat the old block and drive by getting well ahead of the drivers and then exiting the flanks.

You don't see hunters driving standing corn much these days. Either there isn't any corn, there are too few people to mount a drive, or there is too much corn. (Fields tend to be much larger these days than they were twenty-five years ago.)

That is not to say that the block and drive method will not work in other circumstances. Indeed it will, and it is probably the one tactic that every pheasant hunter needs to be aware of, whether it is employed very often or not.

But while driving and blocking can work in other situations, it was really tailor-made for standing corn. Because of the way corn is planted, the fields are perfect for the maneuver. The pheasants have nice little lanes to run in, just like track stars at the Olympics.

Blocking also works quite well in narrow cover, where the

pheasant's options are somewhat limited. My notebooks remind me of one instance where it worked very well and probably provided the blocker with a story he's told many times since.

Jerry Fagle and I were pushing a narrow draw, probably 20 yards across at its widest, through a combined soybean field. The cover in the draw itself was not all that heavy, allowing us to walk on either side while my old pointer, Jake, made sure we didn't pass up any birds.

It was deer season in Iowa, and the blocker, a friend of Jerry's, hadn't yet bagged his buck. Consequently, the blocker, shooting a 12 gauge pump, had a load of 6s in the chamber, backed with several slugs in the magazine. The idea was that he'd use the shot load on any pheasants or shuck it and cut loose with slugs if he had a chance at a deer.

It was quite obvious from Jake's actions that we were moving birds, and it was equally obvious that they weren't likely to hold in the relatively thin cover. As we approached within hailing range of the blocker, I yelled at him to be ready.

Well before we were within range of where the draw dead-ended in the middle of bare ground, a rooster burst out and flew straight at the blocker. He made a nice passing shot.

Then a second bird also flushed his way. Forgetting he had slugs behind the first load of 6s, he cut loose again, dropping the second bird even harder than the first. That second bird, cleanly hit in the air with a slug, was missing about the bottom third of its breast. That's not a load I'd recommend for your normal shots at pheasants.

Because I've hunted regularly with my own dogs for so many years, I've seldom had the opportunity to act as a blocker. I can't really say that I'm sorry, because in spite of exceptions like the one I just mentioned, in my experience the drivers tend to get more shooting. They certainly get most of the chances at birds that realize they're cornered and decide to try to sit it out. When I'm a driver, these usually result in hard points by my dogs and relatively easy shots.

On my only pheasant trip to South Dakota, back in 1979, I was dogless. Well, not exactly—but I knew that I'd be hunting with friends who had *good* dogs, so I left my wild Irish setter at home. My Sauer was also in the shop, and that disturbed me much more than Nick's absence. Just for this trip, I'd purchased a brand new Browning BSS, a handy little 20 with a straight grip, choked improved cylinder and modified. I'd shot it well at woodcock, and although the Iowa pheasant season wasn't open yet, I felt as ready as I could be for South Dakota ringnecks.

On that trip, I found myself in the unaccustomed position of blocker fairly often. The first couple of times, the drivers were working shelterbelts, and the birds were coming out over the treetops. I fired several shots without result and began to blame the gun for my woes. (More likely, I simply wasn't prepared to deal with chances of a kind I'd never seen before. The Sauer's longer barrels and slightly heavier shot charge might have helped a bit, but I just wasn't ready then—and probably am not today, either—for the equivalent of British driven bird shooting.)

Hunkered down behind a weedy fence line, blocking for another drive, I determined to request a chance to do some walking in the next field, dog or no dog. That desire was reinforced by the number of shots I heard fired as the drivers approached.

Then I glanced to my left and spied a cock pheasant trying to slink out under the barbed wire, several fenceposts down. I stood up. He took wing, and that little BSS worked just fine on a shot which was much more familiar to me.

A variation of the block and drive can be used with the cooperation of a friendly farmer. Often, when the last few rows of corn are combined, a surprising number of birds will flush all at once. They do indeed love standing corn, and after they've been living in it and eating it for several weeks, they seem understandably reluctant to leave the security it offers them.

I hunted the opener in 1973 with my father, brother, and nephew. My father had arranged for permission several weeks in advance, and he called ahead the night before to double-check. Fine, said the farmer, and he and Dad agreed that we would simply start our hunt the next morning in a specified field.

What we were dealing with was about 80 acres of corn, perhaps all but 10 of that picked. There were some narrow strips left standing near the road, and we picked up a couple of birds working those in the first half hour or so.

The end of the field farthest from the road contained the bulk of the standing grain. When the farmer showed up with his combine, we'd already worked out all the strips and were making passes back and forth through the picked corn, gradually working toward the large standing plot.

Here, were one to analyze our tactics, we were probably making an error. Novices might think that pheasants cannot run unseen in picked corn, and in so believing, they would be making an understandable, but still very serious, mistake. A rooster pheasant is an imposing bird, standing tall and stretching his long neck. But when he runs, it is often in a crouch with the top of his back not more than 6 inches from the ground.

Thus, what we may well have been doing was pushing birds into the remaining large block of standing corn, which was too big for the four of us to handle. Also, I was working Deke, my Moroccan Brittany, who had a very low tolerance for birds running down cornrows. He was not a good candidate for working standing corn.

The farmer finished off the narrow strips first, and we just happened to complete one of our passes through the picked corn as he came up the fence line, heading for the big plot of corn at the far end of the field.

We showed him the two or three birds we'd collected, and then, typical of friendly Iowa landowners, he made a helpful suggestion.

"Keep an eye on me over there as I finish picking," he said. "Come on and join me when I'm ready to make my last couple of passes. Just walk along beside the combine, and I'll bet you'll get some shooting."

Some farmers still carry shotguns in the cabs of their combines to put a rooster or two in the freezer. This one didn't, and as a result, we put a couple more birds in our game bags.

Another farmer, whose land I've hunted for over ten years now, made me a similar offer. I'd arrived at his place early one afternoon and caught him finishing up the corn in a 40-acre field, bounded on one side by a creek and on the other by a gravel road.

He suggested that I station myself in the ditch across the road from his field, directly in line with the last remaining strip of corn. As has often been the case in my sporadic career as a blocker, the results were nil.

He pulled his combine out on the road. "Can't understand where those birds all went," he said. "I picked half that field today, and I saw at least a dozen of them running around when I first started. Didn't see a one flush."

I sized up the situation. "Maybe I'll try down along the creek," I said.

Jake and I headed into the wide, brushy strip of cover running down one side of the field and ending at the creek. About halfway down, a rooster tried to escape out the far side of the fence. One in the bag. Several others, however, flushed out the end and across the creek before I was in range.

We turned and started working along the creek. There wasn't a lot of cover between the end of the cornrows and the bank, which descended rather abruptly some 15 feet to the fairly substantial stream below.

Jake's actions began to give me the idea that some of the birds may have dropped over the edge. I was about to encourage him down the bank when two roosters flushed. Too eager for a double, I didn't hit the first one hard enough. But the second barrel from the Sauer sent him tumbling into the creek.

The birds in that field hadn't disappeared into thin air after all. Even though the last patch of standing corn had been surrounded by picked grain, the pheasants had managed to slink off into the adjacent cover without the farmer spotting them, even from his excellent vantage point in the combine high above the ground. In the end, I was much happier that he'd pushed them where I could find them with the dog than if he'd flushed them to me out on the road.

As the season wears on, a couple of changes take place in pheasant behavior. They become more and more wary of hunters through repeated and not very pleasant encounters with guns and dogs. They are also likely to bunch up in thicker cover as much of their early fall habitat is eliminated through the course of normal farming practices. Add a fair amount of snow, and you end up with lots of birds in relatively small areas.

The block and drive tactic can be used in such situations, but the participants have to execute the maneuver to perfection. All likely escape routes have to be covered. Perhaps even more importantly, you have to use the element of surprise. Broadcast your approach to a bunch of nervous pheasants, and they are almost certain to vacate the cover before you are within range. My personal opinion is that groups of pheasants are always tougher to work because of the tendency for all of them to fly when one flushes. When the birds have been pushed into ever smaller parcels of cover, they get even harder to work.

Half a dozen of us learned this lesson the hard way on a December hunt in northern Iowa a few years back. We had been hunting for most of the day without much luck. The snow was old and crusted, and although we were moving birds, the roosters in particular all seemed to be flushing beyond range.

When we secured permission to hunt an excellent overgrown pasture with a creek running up the middle, we decided it was time to use a little strategy. We chose a variation of the block and drive—a pincers maneuver. Three of us, myself included, would drop off at one end of the cover. We would approach the hoped-for pheasant sanctuary along a fence line across a quarter mile of barren ground. The other three would drive around to where a bridge crossed the creek and start toward us from there. We agreed that they'd wait until we had crossed the open field.

Our problem was that the other group of three did not recognize the need for stealth. We were about halfway across the field when we saw their station wagon come to a halt right next to the bridge.

"I've got a bad feeling about this," I said quietly to my two partners. "I hope that they wait to get out of the car until we're closer."

My mental telepathy wasn't very good that day. The group at the opposite end definitely did not receive my message. The first slam of a car door was enough to trigger a chain reaction flush, and we were still a long ways from being in position. I did the pheasant hunter's version of the 100-yard dash and got there in time to take the last rooster as he rocketed over my head. But about fifty other birds, including probably a dozen roosters, had preceded him—all flying straight down the cover, right where we would have been in another few minutes.

The other three, chagrined at their mistake when we met in the middle of the now-birdless patch of cover, told us that they hadn't intended to start hunting before we were in place—they were only going to get out and load up. Obviously, we should have emphasized the need for stealth on their end.

Putting a vehicle at one end of a strip of cover will sometimes keep the birds from flushing. However, if there are hunters in the vehicle and they get out within a stone's throw of the cover, the result may well be birds departing before the guns are ever out of their cases. If there are blockers in the vehicle, they should park it at least 100 yards from where they intend to take up position. Even at that distance, they should avoid slamming doors and making too much noise getting into place.

There are a couple of secondary benefits of blocking, even when it does not prove to be effective in trapping birds. The first is that it can save you a lot of unproductive walking. If you are working a narrow strip of cover in the middle of otherwise barren ground, sending one hunter with a vehicle to the far end will spare you the effort of either retracing your steps or taking a long walk across an open field.

The maneuver can also be used to make things a bit easier on hunters who, for whatever reason, aren't in shape for a full day of walking. Allowing them the respite afforded by blocking may be the only way they can keep up with the rest of the group.

Iowa topography lends itself very well to other kinds of blocking or pincers maneuvers, in addition to the classic standing corn drive. For the most part, the state looks like a huge checkerboard when viewed from the air, all neatly laid out in square miles, with gravel roads forming the perimeter of each section. This results in numerous narrow strips of cover a mile long—waterways, fencerows, and railroads, for example. These can be hunted very effectively by two or three hunters with a vehicle. If the cover is narrow enough, it can be about as well designed for the dogless hunter as possible.

One hunter—or two, if the cover is wide enough—start at one end. The other hunter takes the vehicle around to the far side of the mile and either blocks or works back toward his approaching companions. This is an excellent maneuver on railroads, where birds can simply keep running ahead of approaching hunters. Putting someone on the far end can often result in cornering these railway ringnecks.

I spend a good deal of time hunting alone, where there really is not much opportunity to work clever maneuvers. However, I have found one tactic that does put an occasional extra bird in the bag. I call it "reverse logic," for lack of a better name.

Conventional wisdom has it that you should work cover in such a way that you cut off the bird's opportunities to run. The draw that comes to an end in the middle of a field is one example. The waterway which has excellent cover on one farmer's ground but has been cultivated right up to its banks on the adjacent farm is another. You push to where the cover ends, and somewhere near that end, at least one or two roosters should sit tight.

That approach works well early in the season. Eventually, however, the birds become accustomed to hunters coming after them from the same direction. Try going against the conventional wisdom, pushing back into the cover. Logic may tell you that you are working the birds so that they can run on you, but the novelty of the approach seems to confuse them, at least occasionally.

Working this tactic in Iowa usually means approaching along a barren fencerow or across an open field to reach your destination, then pushing back out to a road ditch. Get ready when you hit the ditch. Although it often has good cover, and the birds could easily turn either left or right and keep running, they frequently elect to sit tight instead. My dogs and I love it when they do.

Hunters with dogs are often well advised to forget about tactics entirely. The best and most obvious approach as you see it may not be the best way to use your dog to its greatest advantage. I always try to hunt the most productive looking cover into the wind, regardless of whether or not this seems logical.

Using the wind to your advantage is especially important in dry conditions, when birds are tough for the dog to find. Give your dog every opportunity to use its nose to the greatest effect.

Hunting into the wind can be useful even for the dogless hunter. Wind makes birds jumpy, and it will carry the sounds of even a relatively stealthy lone hunter a surprising distance—especially to the sharp ears of a skulking pheasant. Using the wind to conceal your approach may well allow you to surprise the same birds that would never let you get within range if you came at them with the wind behind you.

Working slowly and thoroughly in heavy cover, with or without a dog, is also preferable to charging through the brush at breakneck speed. In thick stuff, even a good dog needs to take its time. One reason is that, if the birds are not moving much, there are a lot of potential hiding spots which must be checked out. If you are into a lot of birds which are moving, the dog may lock onto one and trail it. As a result, you and the dog may well walk by others that are hiding.

How many times have you almost stepped on a bird when your dog was off hunting intently somewhere else? This is often not the dog's fault. Quail hang out in nice, tight coveys. Grouse are found quite scattered, for the most part. If you are into a flight, you can move a lot of woodcock in a relatively small area, but they don't really move around all that much on the ground, leaving all kinds of confusing scents for your dog.

Pheasants, on the other hand, can be found in quite large, but very loosely knit, bunches. Just try to sort out tracks, even if the snow is fresh, in a piece of cover inhabited by a lot of birds. This is more or less what your dog is trying to do with scent, which is why it may appear to miss birds. In fact, you've probably found one that it just hasn't gotten around to yet. Give your dog the time it needs to work the cover.

Rushing through cover behind a dog may be justified if the cover is relatively thin and if it is apparent that the birds are running. In such a situation, you are probably better off hustling after the dog and hoping that you get close enough for a shot.

I want to end this chapter where I began it. Tactics can be effective in certain situations. But most of the time, following a good dog in good cover is the only tactic you really need to put birds in the bag.

Hunting Companions

HEASANT hunting seems to have been born as a group sport. In this it differs from many other types of hunting, even most other varieties of upland bird hunting. Grouse and woodcock tend to be pursued by a lone hunter and his dog, or at most by a pair of gunners. The same is true of bobwhites.

During the heyday of the pheasant in the Midwest, the cornfield drive was the accepted way of hunting ringnecks. Many of these operations were carried out in quasi-military style and encompassed at least a squad, if not a full platoon, of bird-hunting infantry.

While the upper crust of the bird-hunting fraternity may look upon driven bird shooting in Europe as the epitome of the sport, they took a decidedly different view—directly down their noses—at the Midwest equivalent. Maybe it was because the overall-wearing "beaters" carried guns, or maybe it was because dogs, with the exception of an occasional cur from the farmyard who functioned as a retriever, played no role. In any case, American pheasants and pheasant hunting of that era were much like Rodney Dangerfield—lacking in the respect department.

Such large-group hunting is mostly a thing of the past, and I can't say that I mourn its passing. I was not yet an ardent pheasant hunter when the tactic faded from popularity. Dad, who had the opportunity to participate in such maneuvers with groups of his John Deere co-workers, preferred not to. I grew up hunting with a small team, which usually consisted of Dad, my older brother, Errol, and myself.

As I explained earlier, Dad was a confirmed road hunter. My first initiation to the identification of pheasant cover came from the rear window of a 1948 Dodge sedan, traveling down gravel roads at modest speeds. On these early undertakings, my mother was also a frequent companion, and I marveled at her ability to spot birds in the ditch.

It got to be a game, with me trying to outspot Mother. As far as I can remember, I never won. At first, I concentrated on the ditch on my side of the car—usually the driver's side, because Dad needed to pay at least some attention to the business of staying on the road. Then I began to notice that Dad and Mother reacted differently, depending on the cover in and adjacent to the ditch. Where the ditch was good and weedy, and especially where there was corn on the other side of the fence, Dad would slow down and Mother's pheasant-finding radar would intensify its search. When ditches were bare, and when farmsteads were too close at hand, Dad picked up speed and Mother relaxed her vigilance.

Thus I learned, well before I ever carried a gun afield, what kind of cover pheasants prefer. Dad explained it all to me in some detail as we scouted the back roads.

On occasion, when a ditch looked especially promising, and particularly when fresh snow showed pheasant tracks, Dad would stop, get out and "tromp" the ditch. As an eager lad, after I felt we'd been sitting too long without sufficient activity, I'd often ask him if we could stop to "tromp" a little. I soon discovered that his preference for doing most of his hunting from the car had nothing to do with any lack of ability to walk the cover. Until he hit 60 or so, Dad could walk with the best of them.

Opening day was different. Dad always secured permission to hunt at least one farm, well in advance of that magic day in November. On one of those occasions, he'd nailed down the rights to a place not far from our home in Waterloo that just happened to have one of the most likely looking pieces of cover around. A medium-sized creek and adjacent low-lying, grassy cover—locally known as a slough—was the jewel on this particular farm, and that was where we started our hunt.

There was a heavy dew that morning, and the weeds were wet. Dad chose to do his walking in his hip boots, about which Errol and I were quick to chide him. He was pushing 60 then, and we didn't want him to handicap himself on a long day's hunt with a couple of eager fellows in their twenties.

The creek meandered back and forth through the cover, with

most of the grass sometimes on one side, sometimes on the other. Eventually, we reached a spot where we either had to cross the creek or leave Dad alone on the far side to hunt a 100-yard-wide strip of grass, without the aid of a dog.

The creek was too wide to jump and too deep to wade in hunting boots. Dad calmly strolled over to the stream, unloaded his gun, left it on the bank, and waded across in his hip boots. He then carried us across piggyback, one at a time. We didn't say anything more about his hip boots for the rest of the day.

Although I hunted squirrels and rabbits with Dad, pheasants were really what he preferred, and he passed that attitude on to me. We didn't hunt any other birds. He wasn't a waterfowler, there were no quail nearby, and grouse and woodcock were not yet legal game in Iowa.

Dad gets credit for instilling in his son a love of hunting. An appreciation for good dogs, fine guns, and a slightly more ethical way of taking birds came from other sources, primarily the outdoor writers whose articles I read during my formative years.

Dad never saw a good pheasant dog work until I took him along on a preserve hunt, where Jake put on quite a show for him. Dad was well past 70 at the time and had stopped hunting a few years earlier. He was still plenty fit to walk, and he swears to this day that Jake was the smartest dog in the world. "That was really something, the way he found every one of those birds," he still says, every time he recalls the day. I only wish that I had passed him my double and let him shoot one.

Truthfully, however, I'm not sure he would have felt comfortable with that gun. Dad did most of his hunting with a break-open .410 single, barrel worn thin, bead sight missing, and forearm taped to the barrel. Errol, Mother, and I pooled our resources one year and bought him a J. C. Higgins bolt-action .410 for Christmas. Although he used it a lot, I think it was mostly to humor us. He treated it like a Purdey, but I've always secretly suspected that he preferred his old single shot.

My brother was the other hunting companion of my early years, but he was much more of a fisherman. In fact, he was much more of a team sport enthusiast (especially softball, which he played for years and still coaches) than an outdoorsman. But we still had some interesting experiences.

Dad bought him a Stevens .410 single when he was about 14. Errol is eight years my senior, and by the time I was ready for a gun of my own, he was pretty well out of hunting and passed his down to me as a present. In fact, that gun passed back and forth between us a couple of times in each direction. When I had it and he was gunless, Errol would simply borrow one of Dad's two guns.

Like Dad, Errol preferred shooting them on the ground. I expect that he also had a good appreciation of the limitations of a .410. I, on the other hand, kept trying to do with it what the writers described doing with larger bores, and ones with more than one shot at that.

We had one near disaster when a flushing rooster caught us both by surprise on a cold day. We were within about 10 feet of one another. Encumbered with gloves, I managed to touch off the little gun before I was quite ready—either the hammer fell before it reached full cock and detonated the shell or else my finger slapped the trigger before I had the gun fully to shoulder. (Most of those hammer guns have a real hair trigger—one reason why they are not the best choices for youngsters.) In either case, the report gave Errol severe ringing in his ears for the rest of the day. Had the muzzle been just a bit farther in his direction, the result could have been tragic. That incident remains as close as I have come to disaster afield.

As a teenager, Errol's son Randy gave every indication of being more interested in hunting than his father. Dad and I bought him a youth-model 20 gauge for Christmas one year, and I gave him some instruction on the skeet range, as well as taking him along pheasant hunting with me. I may have dampened his enthusiasm, if you will forgive the pun, when I sent him across overly thin creek ice to follow fresh tracks in the new snow. My sister-in-law wasn't terribly understanding about it but at least credited my good sense for bringing him home to dry out.

By that time, I'd graduated from the Stevens .410, which I passed back to Errol so he could go along with me and Randy. Like Dad, Errol had virtually no experience with bird dogs. We were working opposite sides of a railroad right-of-way, and Deke had chosen to work in front of Errol. They were out of sight because of the elevated track bed between us, and we kept in touch by calling back and forth frequently.

"Hey, Deke's stopped and won't move," Errol called. I didn't have time to explain to him what that meant before the bird came cackling up in front of him. I tried scrambling up to the tracks where I could get a shot, but as luck would have it, the bird went the wrong way.

"Couldn't get the hammer back," he explained, half laughing and half frustrated. Deke, who had little success getting pheasants to hold for his points, probably saw no humor in it whatsoever.

Neither Dad nor Errol ever developed my passion for bird hunting. They did, however, start me out right, by giving me a gun and seeing to it that I didn't shoot myself or anyone else. Despite the fact that my diaries don't start until 1973, my memories of those early family hunts, in the late 1950s and early 1960s, are still among the most vivid.

Next to owning a good dog and shooting a gun that fits with loads that will stop pheasants, one of the key ingredients to successful and enjoyable pheasant hunting is good companions. When I returned to the States in 1973, with my first real bird dog and a passion to try him out on pheasants, neither my dad nor my brother hunted much anymore. But through a pure stroke of luck, I stumbled upon a hunting companion with whom I've spent a lot of great days afield over the past fifteen years.

Mike Carroll and I were graduate students together. One day over a beer, I happened to mention grouse and woodcock hunting—a sport I'd just taken up, thanks to a heavy dose of George Bird Evans. Mike indicated a strong interest in giving it a try.

On our first hunt together, I recall being duly impressed when Mike uncased a nice Winchester 101 20 gauge. Grad students attending school on the GI Bill didn't shoot guns like that unless they were fairly serious hunters. It didn't take me long to find out how serious Mike was or to what lengths he would go to protect that precious superposed.

On one of our first grouse hunts, back before we determined that you couldn't really hunt grouse if the ridges were so steep that you couldn't put both feet down to shoot, Mike took a nasty tumble and went sliding down a rocky hillside. He would have stopped himself much sooner, and done much less damage to his body, had he not been so worried about his gun that he held it aloft with one hand throughout the course of his rather unusual descent. The gun ended up unscratched, which is a lot more than I can say for Mike.

The only drawback to our partnership in its initial stages was that Mike shot woodcock pretty well, and I didn't shoot them well at all. Fortunately, I managed to even things up a bit more when pheasant season rolled around.

My old Brittany, Deke, who had been trained in French, even caused Mike to pick up a smattering of the tongue. Deke appreciated the effort and returned the favor by spending a lot of

Mike Carroll of Hudson, Iowa, a hunting companion for over fifteen years.

nights using Mike's old wool jacket as a bed in the back of the station wagon.

Hunting with Mike caused me to change some of my personal habits. I went through a period where I was notoriously forgetful, locking my keys in the car on two or three occasions. Once, Mike succeeded in beating on a wing with a rock until the catch gave. Another time, he finally managed to convice me that I should carry a spare key in my wallet.

We'd just hunted a railroad on a particularly cold day—wind-chill well below zero. We hadn't even seen a pheasant track. When we got back to the car, an old Pontiac Tempest that semed more than a little jinxed in the first place, both of us cased our guns and tossed them and our jackets in the trunk. As soon as I shut it, I realized that my keys were in the jacket pocket.

I explained the dilemma to Mike, suggested that I walk to the nearest farmhouse, about half a mile away, and call my wife, who was some 50 miles away, to come to the rescue. Mike glanced around, the wind whistling through his thin flannel shirt. "You don't need to do that."

Before I could object, Mike had ripped a metal fencepost out of the ground and was using it as a pry-bar on the trunk. I think that I stood there with my mouth open through the whole epi-sode, which didn't last long, because Mike made quick work of the trunk. It didn't work too well after that, but I didn't keep the car for long either. I haven't been caught without a spare key since then.

Perfect hunting partners are people in roughly the same physical shape as you are, with hunting ethics similar to your own. They don't criticize your dog overly much, even when it deserves it. They'll either offer to drive or chip in some gas money. They won't eat half your lunch, at least not without of-fering you half of theirs. They won't claim every bird that both of you happen to shoot at. They may razz you a bit over an easy miss, but they'll know to lay off if you're in the doldrums of a slump.

Partners like that are hard to find. Mike is all of those things, and a lot more.

Like me, Mike doesn't believe in party shooting. He'd rather take his own chances at the roosters. Back in 1987, on opening day, I'd shot quite well and took my three birds before noon. By then, a cold rain was falling. I worked Heidi with Mike, carrying my gun to back him up in case of a cripple. After a half hour of getting wet and not moving birds, Mike stopped and turned to me. "Let's call it a day," he said. "I had chances at more than my three-bird limit, and just didn't make the shots. No use ruining a good day by getting ourselves soaked."

My boy Matt and Mike's son Josh are the same age, and both are just starting to hunt. I only hope that they can grow to have the same kind of partnership their fathers have had, one where the sport and the memories are more important than the number of birds in the bag.

Outdoor writers are an interesting bunch of people. Few of them are experts at everything, but the ones I've gotten to know well have been pretty fair pheasant hunters. Perhaps it's like the old "birds of a feather" proverb—except in this case, it happened to be writers with the same passion flocking together to hunt pheasants.

Steve Grooms, Tom Huggler, Gene Kroupa, and I all wrote for the same magazine back in the late 1970s. I met them at a conference the magazine organized, and for whatever foolish reason invited all three to come to Iowa for a pheasant hunt. We didn't really know one another all that well, but what could have been a disaster turned out quite well. The birds cooperated nicely, and the four of us managed not to get on each others' nerves over the course of the hunt.

I'd lined up several good farms for that group hunt. It was Thanksgiving week, the birds were shell-shocked veterans, and I knew we'd need a lot of good territory to provide really quality hunting for four hard-charging scattergunners. We'd also made reservations at a motel in the area we were hunting.

I got there first, only to take a call from Huggler, who told me that Grooms had an emergency of some kind and that he was still with Kroupa in Wisconsin tracking down a wounded deer. As it turned out, Huggler was making the call from the motel lobby. Fortunately for him, he didn't waste much time getting to the room. I was already on the phone, dialing some of my local friends to pinch-hit for these out-of-staters who were going to miss out on the blue-ribbon ringneck hunt. That joke almost backfired.

From then on, things got better. The only negative aspect of the whole hunt was my idiot Irish setter, Nick, who was doing a great job of finding birds 100 yards away, then flushing and chasing them. He spent most of the hunt in the car.

The other three had great dogs. Grooms's springer, Brandy, and Kroupa's Lab, Briar, were both in their primes. Huggler was running a yearling English setter bitch named Brinka, who tried hard for rookie of the year honors with a number of classic points.

The shooting was pretty fancy, too. On the second day of the hunt, joined by a local friend of mine, the five of us shot at fourteen roosters and bagged thirteen of them. Grooms, probably the best shot of the bunch, missed the first bird of the day.

Dave Prine, another of Larry Brown's hunting companions.

Actually, however, the chances of such a hunt working out are not all that great. You have four experienced pheasant hunters who have never hunted together, using both pointing and flushing dogs. You can end up with four different ideas about how you ought to hunt, four different codes of ethics, four different opinions about dividing up expenses, etc. That's not really the way to organize a pheasant hunting team, especially when you're going to be hunting together for several days. Better to bring one new person at a time into a group, and then, if possible, on a one-day hunt rather than a long-distance safari. Sure, you can make new friends by taking them along on a trip, but you're also jeopardizing the whole experience if you've invited a newcomer that none of the "old hands" have hunted with before.

I first teamed up with Dave Prine back in 1983, after he had beaten me—and everyone else—in the previous winter's Iowa-Illinois Pheasant Hunting Championship. I was doing an article on hard-core pheasant hunters, guys who bag forty or fifty birds per season or more consistently. Since I've known Dave, he's never bagged fewer than fifty birds in a season, and he's topped the seventy mark a couple of times.

Although those numbers are pretty staggering to most pheasant shooters, Dave is no game hog. He is one of the most ethical guys I've ever had the pleasure of joining in the field. He shoots classic American side-by-sides, owning all of the Big Three—Parker, L. C. Smith, Fox. He has a sporting library that would be the envy of most bird hunters.

Dave just happens to be one of those lucky guys who has a lot of spare time during pheasant season. He's a grain farmer, and once the crops are harvested, Dave hunts. He takes a brief break from pheasants during the Iowa shotgun deer season in early December, and then it's back to the birds. He's lived in Mahaska County for all of his life and knows virtually every landowner by first name.

We had our first hunt together in December 1983. That was the year of the Payment in Kind (PIK) Program, one of those one-year Washington wonders that was supposed to solve all the grain surplus woes. Farmers did indeed respond to PIK, taking millions of acres out of corn production. Much of it grew up to excellent pheasant cover. The only problem was that the grain surplus evaporated almost overnight, and the following year it was back to business as usual. But in defense of PIK, it did produce some excellent short-term benefits for pheasant hunters.

Dave and I started our hunt in a 20-acre patch of PIK foxtail, working behind his big black Lab, Luke. We hit the field at 8:15 and had our six birds by 8:45. Not a bad hunt, cosidering the season was half over. At one point, we took a two-man double—each of us had a rooster dead in the air at the same time.

We've hunted together quite a few times since then, and we've taken quite a few limits, but none quite as quick as that first one. I think it's also the only time I've ever outshot Dave. I was three for three on that hunt, and Dave missed a couple of times. He is an excellent clay bird shot and doesn't miss pheasants very often.

Dave and I share a love of good side-by-side shotguns, good dogs, good sporting literature, and pheasants. I've shown him some fine grouse and woodcock shooting, including a trip to Michigan's Upper Peninsula, and he's shown me a lot of fine pheasant shooting in Mahaska County. Swapping hunts like that is also an excellent way to develop a partnership, although I'd be a little leery of it on the basis of an ad in a magazine with someone I've never met.

Chuck Gates is a gunsmith from Brooklyn, Iowa, with whom I've also enjoyed many fine hunts. Chuck had the rather dubious honor of fixing my old Sauer the last time the top lever broke. Like Dave Prine, Chuck is a fellow who's lived most of his life in one area and thus has the distinct advantage of knowing most of the surrounding landowners. Having access to a lot of places to hunt is a real plus to a pheasant chaser.

Chuck and I also happen to own a couple of dogs that hunt very well together, another key ingredient of a successful hunting partnership. His shorthair, Smokey, makes a good match with my Heidi. In fact, we've planned on mating them for some time, but things never seem to have worked out.

We only had about one decent snowfall during the 1987 season, and Chuck and I had the good fortune to be out right after it. We hit a farm which had been placed in the Conservation Reserve Program (CRP), which, like PIK, produced a lot of good cover, with the added advantage of being a ten-year, rather than a one-year, program.

That farm was in almost solid cover of one sort or another, mostly grass and weeds from knee to waist high. The birds had roosted beneath the thick stuff, and had it not been for the dogs, we would have had trouble finding and flushing them. As it was, most came over solid points. Some sat so tight that we actually walked by them in the deep snow and would have gone on had the dogs not insisted that a bird was there.

My notebook reveals about equal numbers of points and backs by both dogs, with Chuck and me taking turns shooting. We took about two hours to take our two-man limit, with the dogs working very cautiously in the heavy snow and thick cover.

Athough I enjoy good company on a pheasant hunt, I actually end up doing quite a bit of my hunting alone. Over the last several years, I've either worked full time at writing or had a flexible teaching schedule. In either case, it gives me a lot of time during the week, when most people with "normal" jobs are at work.

One hunter with a good dog can work pheasants quite effectively if they confine themselves to cover that doesn't overwhelm them. I do a lot of my solo hunting on narrow creeks and draws, where a dog and I can cover everything worth hunting without difficulty.

Another advantage of hunting solo is that you don't have to

Two generations of hunting partners—Chuck Gates and his son, Josh. Their shorthair, Smokey, is Heidi's favorite four-legged companion.

find many birds to have a successful hunt. When it's past mid-season and the birds have wised up, if I'm out alone and get one good chance at a rooster in a couple of hours, I'm very pleased—especially when the dog works the bird well. If I'm hunting with a partner or two, I know that everyone would like to have at least one good opportunity, which means we have to find that many more birds.

Another advantage to hunting alone, especially later in the season when the birds are hunter-wise, is that you can do so without a lot of noise. I try not to talk a lot while working birds anyhow, but just a couple of quiet exchanges between partners can spook them if the birds are really nervous. When I'm alone, the only sounds are the dog's bell and, if I need to control the dog, my whistle. I don't think either alarms birds like voices do.

A solo hunter also stands a much better chance of gaining permission to hunt. I've often had farmers come to the door and, in response to my request to hunt, ask how many are with me, glancing warily at my pickup. When I explain that it's just me and a dog, I very seldom get turned away. In many cases, there is a bit of hesitation, and I'm sure that the farmer feels a lone hunter, who isn't likely to take more than a bird or two, is a much better risk than two or three hunters, let alone five or six.

Despite the advantages of solo hunting, I'll still take at least one good companion in almost any situation. My son, Matt, just turning a teenager, is showing definite promise of being one of my future companions. I hope that I can do as well teaching him as Dad did teaching me.

Pheasants I Have Known

LTHOUGH much more praise has been heaped upon the ruffed grouse and the bobwhite quail, I find pheasants to have more individuality. You can make some accurate generalizations about ringnecks, but there are individual birds that don't fit the mold and which, at least for me, stand out clearly through my more than three decades of gunning pheasants.

There is one generalization, however, which every pheasant hunter knows to be true. Among our most popular game birds, the rooster pheasant is the one that takes a licking and keeps on ticking. I've seen birds hit three times in the air and somehow they manage to keep flying. Often, if you are able to mark them down, they can be found not far from where they land.

My most recent notebook reminds me of one such bird. I had just crossed a creek, and when the bird flushed, it rose more abruptly than normal to clear the top of the bank. At least that's the best excuse I can give for my low first shot. Feathers flew everywhere, and the bird started to drop. In those cases, I almost always throw my second shot high, and this time was no exception.

The bank screened the bird's flight path from then on, but I scrambled up behind Heidi, hoping that the bird would drop. About 100 yards down a fence line, Heidi went on point. The bird hobbled off in a weak attempt to escape, but didn't get far. When I cleaned that pheasant, I was amazed it had been able to move at all. Both legs were broken.

Chuck Gates's youngest son, Josh, had the same thing hap-

135

pen to him while hunting with his father and me. He hit a rooster hard but low, and the bird sailed at least a couple hundred yards before we marked it down near the junction of two small creeks.

We followed the bird's line of flight. Just before reaching the junction, we spotted our two shorthairs on point. "Here's your bird," called Chuck. When he kicked into the dense creekbank cover, however, the rooster came busting out in a surprisingly healthy manner. Chuck and I cut short the bird's flight.

"I don't think that was your bird, Josh," said Chuck as Smokey delivered the rooster to him. "It flew too well, and neither leg seems broken." We had all observed at least one leg dangling on the bird Josh had hit.

About that time, I noticed Heidi's absence. Chuck said he'd seen her head on down the creek. I couldn't hear her bell and walked the short distance to where the two creeks joined. Dropping down to the frozen stream, I found two sets of tracks—one dog, one pheasant—in the skiff of fresh snow on the ice.

I continued to follow the tracks, and a bit farther on, I spotted Heidi pointing intensely into the weeds next to the ice. I kicked into the cover, but nothing happened. Then Heidi dove in and emerged with a very much alive but wounded pheasant.

"Here's your bird, Josh," I said, clambering up the steep bank with the rooster in hand. With two broken legs, that bird had still covered quite a bit of distance before Heidi found it.

That same season, Gary Bergmann, who shoots a pump, hit one bird three times only to watch it sail away. Fortunately, we were also able to mark it down. But unlike Josh Gates's bird, this one did not give us any handy reference point to work from. It landed in a fairly wide and featureless field of grass.

Once again, Heidi's nose was invaluable. Had she not pointed that bird, I doubt we ever would have recovered it. Her point, however, was not very intense, which is not at all typical of her performance. The bird was so badly crippled that it just sat there while I reached down to pick it up, and I can only assume that she sensed it as being more dead than alive.

I've already described the phenomenon of pheasants that fly on after being hit and then suddenly drop dead from the sky. As I mentioned earlier, that happened to both birds in the only true double I've ever taken, and I was extremely lucky to recover both of them.

Grouse hunters in particular report a strange behavior they call "towering," where a wounded bird flies straight up for some distance and then drops like a rock. Personally, I've never experienced it, but a number of reliable observers mention having seen more than one grouse tower.

Dr. Charles Norris, whose book *Eastern Upland Shooting* is a classic, shot a lot of pheasants in the Middle Atlantic states from the time they were introduced, early in this century, into the 1950s. He reports having seen quail tower, as well as grouse, but never pheasants. I have never seen a pheasant tower, nor has anyone else I know of.

One bird that kept going with a mortal wound put me in a strange situation from an ethical standpoint. It happened in 1989, an excellent pheasant season during which I bagged sixty-three roosters. I did a lot of hunting that year on CRP ground, and three or four of those set-aside farms I hunted seemed to have unbelievable numbers of birds.

I went to teach my classes that morning with Rebel in the dog box, and after changing into hunting clothes and letting her stretch her legs a bit, we were on the road. We reached our destination about 1:45, and I was looking forward to a short, but hopefully productive, afternoon hunt. It turned out to be shorter than I expected, and more productive than I wanted.

Reb started making game before I had shells in the gun. The birds were moving a bit, but we trapped the first against a fence separating the heavy set-aside cover from an open, combined soybean field. The bird flushed angling away from me, and Reb squeezed under the fence to make the retrieve on the easy shot.

Bird number two found itself similarly pinned against a fence with no more room to run, this time with a pond surrounded by shortgrass pasture on the other side of the barbed wire. My shot was not fatal, but Reb caught the runner before he could make it back into heavy cover.

The bird which should have given me my limit came over a hard point, and it flushed going straight away. The first shot struck hard but low, and once again I felt that the second shot had gone high as the bird dropped from the hit. Then it seemed to regain its momentum and sailed out of sight over a hill. Although Reb went after it, I had little hope in that dense sea of wall-to-wall cover, and she came back birdless.

Ten minutes later, I'd all but forgotten that bird as Reb retrieved the rooster I needed to limit out, an easy shot over another point. I glanced at my watch and noted that the whole affair had taken a bit over half an hour.

My only course back to the pickup was through more excellent cover, most of which we hadn't worked, so I was hardly sur-

Late-season birds often hang out in dense cover. This season-ending bird came from the cattails behind Larry Brown.

prised when Reb locked up again. With a limit in my vest, I put down my gun and got out the camera for a few close-ups of the dog on point.

I snapped several shots, and by the time I took the last one, I was close enough to Reb to be surprised that the bird was still holding. I looked closer and saw a dead rooster right under her nose. I picked it up and discovered it was the bird I had hit previously, several hundred yards away from where it had flushed and at quite an angle from the line it had been flying when it went out of sight.

Dead birds, even recently killed ones, don't put out a lot of scent, and it was an incredible piece of luck to find that rooster in all that cover. Then I realized my dilemma: that was my fourth bird. I thought about leaving it where I'd found it, but for me that goes against the grain. I was over the limit, but it was an honest mistake, and although I didn't like to think about the possibility of being stopped by a game warden, my conscience was relatively clear. Another hunter might have stopped after two birds in the bag and a third hit, assuming the last one would die. In this case, that would have been an even more appropriate course than the one I chose. However, I've seen plenty of pheasants carry off a lot of shot, and I've shot plenty of others carrying someone else's pellets and not appearing much the worse for it.

As I've already stated, I have only one true double on pheasants to my credit, and although my notebooks mention a couple of occasions where I've missed chances at doubles, they have been relatively rare in my experience. Because of a pheasant's ability to carry shot, hunters should be cautious about taking doubles. The problem is that most of us have trouble resisting such an opportunity, and instinct takes over before our brain has time to consider such things as the density of the cover or the location of the dog. Either or both of these factors have a lot to do with the success of retrieving a double, even when the gunner succeeds in knocking both birds down.

There are days when you walk and walk, and opportunities simply do not present themselves. Then there are the other days, when it all happens almost too quickly.

Two high school classmates of mine, Jim Cole and Doug Carpenter, had invited me to join them for a hunt near Denison in western Iowa. Never having hunted that area before, but having heard good things about the bird population, I was eager to give it a try.

The first day of the weekend hunt was cold and windy, and we struck out totally in the morning. Things did pick up a bit in the afternoon. I dropped two birds over solid points by Heidi along brushy creeks. We finished the day in a large set-aside field, where Rebel found several pheasants. Unfortunately, Jim and I missed one easy chance, and I wing-tipped one that escaped when a woven wire fence cut off Rebel's pursuit. Finally, Doug dropped one just about at the end of legal shooting hours over Reb's nice point.

Our local guide, Vic Thomsen, took us along Paradise Creek the next morning. The name turned out to be an appropriate one. Doug was walking a high bank on one side, while Heidi, Vic, his son Greg, and I worked the other side, which had most of the good cover.

We'd cut across to our side in pursuit of a bird that had flushed wild. The ditch along a gravel road—within gunshot of the creek in most places, depending on twists and turns—produced a point by Heidi on a bird that was not at all excited about moving and a kill for Vic.

Then Doug summoned me back from the other side. "There's some good cover on your bank," he called. "I think you'd better take Heidi through it."

The ditch bank blocked my view, but as I angled back to the creek, I saw what Doug meant. A sandy little peninsula, choked with willows and brush, jutted out into the stream.

Heidi no more than had her nose into the cover when two birds broke out, one right and one left. Leaving the right-hand bird to Doug, I drew down on the other, dropping him on the high bank across the creek, well in front of my partner.

Doug was still looking the other way, at the bird which had managed to escape him. I broke the gun, dropped a fresh shell in the right barrel, and yelled, "You've got a dead bird down in front of you. Heidi's coming across."

I took a step forward and another rooster flushed straight away from me. I dropped it hard on my own side. As I brought my gun down, another bird came crashing out of the willows, headed on a similar line to the first bird I'd killed. My left barrel took this one, which didn't quite clear the high bank on the far side. It rolled a ways down the dirt embankment, coming to rest about halfway between the top of the bank and the creek.

That entire sequence—three birds dead, and all of them stayed exactly where they hit—took less than thirty seconds. It is by far the fastest I have ever killed a limit, but it did not include a true double.

Heidi, bringing back my first bird from the far side, nearly stepped on the third one as she came down the bank. Looking a bit bewildered, she paused briefly as if trying to figure out how to get two of them in her mouth, then decided it couldn't be done and brought me the one she already had.

Greg walked over to where I was standing, his eyes the size of half dollars. Not yet 12 years old, he'd just read an article I'd written about pheasant hunting along creeks. "You sure were right about creeks being good spots!" he said.

All of the above is proof that pheasants can be very hard or very easy, which most pheasant hunters already know. Those with enough years of ringneck chasing under their belts also realize that pheasants can be just plain strange from time to time.

My first really unusual experience with a pheasant goes back to the days before I carried a gun, probably almost forty years ago. I was riding in the old 1948 Dodge with Dad, sitting in the car waiting for him to come back from a brief "tromp" along a road ditch.

As he approached the car, I noticed that he had a rooster in hand. Curious because I hadn't heard a shot, I asked what happened.

"Somebody must have crippled this bird," he replied. "I stepped on it in the weeds, but it couldn't fly. I just picked it up and banged its head on a fencepost."

Both of us were quite surprised, upon returning home, to find the bird sitting up and giving us the pheasant version of the evil eye from a corner of the car trunk. Dad took the bird down to the basement, where we cleaned all our game. Perhaps through fear, or perhaps through the strangeness of the surroundings, the bird seemed to lose all its instinct to avoid people. The big rooster, apparently only wing-broken, strutted around, checking everything out, quite oblivious to our presence.

Cleaning a bird that was already dead was one thing. Killing one that was strolling innocently around was quite another. I suggested to Dad that we keep it as a pet, but he explained to me that the game wardens would frown on such things. Having become too well acquainted with that bird, I had to leave the scene of the crime before Dad dispatched him.

My second close encounter with an overly healthy pheasant came about the time I finished high school. School chum Larry Forsyth and I were bird hunting in deep snow. As we walked along, focusing on the ground for tracks (we were hunting dogless), I noticed a set of rooster tailfeathers protruding from the snow right between my feet. There were no tracks around, and I made the logical assumption.

"Look at this," I called to Larry, reaching down to pick up the feathers. "Someone got a . . ."

I never finished that sentence. Just as I grabbed the feathers, a very live bird flushed, attached to the other end of the tail, showering me in snow. Both of us shot and missed. All I had to show for it were the bird's two longest feathers, which he'd left in my hand in his haste to depart. Either he'd flown directly into the snow and stayed there, or else freshly fallen snow had covered his tracks—and everything else, except his tail. In either case, he was safe but sporting a somewhat less magnificent set of plumage.

The second time a pheasant's tail gave away its presence, I was much more cautious, as a result of that experience. My brother Errol, nephew Randy, and I were returning home from a hunt. As we drove down the highway, we spotted a group of hunters some distance from us in an adjacent field.

Several birds flushed in front of them. I watched as one bird, clearly hit, sailed across the road and landed in the ditch on the opposite side.

"Stop the car!" I told my brother abruptly. I explained to him what had happened. By this time we were some distance beyond the spot where I'd marked the bird, so he made a U-turn and headed back down the road.

I was sure that I had the bird marked within about 20 or 30 yards one way or the other. I suggested that we all take our guns, in case it was still able to fly or run, and cover the area. The hunters across the road from us apparently hadn't seen the bird come down and had headed off in the opposite direction.

The ditch had several inches of light snow, and I figured that finding the bird would be a cinch. But after working down the ditch, far beyond where I'd marked him, and back again, we hadn't seen a track. It was near zero, and the wind was blowing hard. Both Randy and Errol headed back to the car.

"I'm going to make one more try," I said. "That bird can't have disappeared."

This time, looking extra hard for tracks, blood, or any other sign, I focused my efforts on the fence which separated the ditch from the adjacent field. The fence line was where I thought the bird had landed, and because it had some clumps of weedy cover, that seemed the most logical place for the bird to hide.

About half a dozen fenceposts after starting my search, I spotted two footprints, and what at first glance appeared to be a weed sticking from the snow. Closer examination showed it to be tailfeathers.

My dilemma now was that the feathers barely protruded through my side of the fence. The bird was just on the other side. The three-strand fence was just high enough that I couldn't step over it. The last thing I wanted was to have that bird catch me with one foot on the bottom strand of wire, the other suspended somewhere in space. If it could take wing again, it would surely escape if I were in such a position.

I tried kicking and throwing snow on the bird, shouting "Hey, get out of there!" for good measure. No result.

Gingerly, I knelt down, reaching for the tailfeathers with my left hand and keeping my gun as ready as I could in my right. Maybe the bird had made it that far and died.

I gave the tailfeathers a pull. The rooster pulled the other way but this time was unable to fly. But both legs were apparently quite healthy, and I took him on the ground as he raced across the snow.

The length of a rooster's tail is often used as a measure of the bird's age or its quality as a "trophy." Many sporting goods stores in pheasant country run annual tailfeather contests.

In my experience, a bird with a tail 2 feet long is quite rare. The longest tail feather I've ever collected measured 25¼ inches and came from a big rooster that had no spurs at all. You could see spots on his legs where the spurs belonged, but he didn't even have the little "bumps" typical of some juveniles. I have always wondered whether that bird never developed spurs, or whether he broke them off fighting or through some other type of accident. The latter would seem a more likely possibility if only one of the two spurs had been missing.

Long, black spurs and a long tail usually go together and are a good indication that the bird is in at least his second season. My spurless bird was an obvious exception to this rule. A bird I shot on Christmas Eve day in 1989, in a heavily wooded public hunting area along the Des Moines River, was an exception of a different sort. He sported the long, pointed spurs of a veteran, but his tail barely measured 20 inches.

But top prize for the most unusual bird of my hunting career had nothing to do with its tail or spurs. I remember it so clearly because of the circumstances surrounding our encounter.

I was hunting near Anamosa in eastern Iowa with fellow French teacher Denny Conrad. My canine assistant at the time was Nick the Red Rocket, my legendary Irish setter, who had been behaving so badly that he didn't make the trip.

Hunting dogless, Denny and I were on opposite sides of a narrow creek. We were within gunshot of a fence that crossed the creek ahead of us when a rooster flushed about 10 yards in front of me.

As I brought the old Sauer to my shoulder, the bird hit the top strand of the fence, somersaulted, and landed hard on its back on the opposite side.

I hustled up to the fence, where I was confronted with the sight of the bird lying on its back in open pasture on the far side, feet in the air, either dead or very badly stunned.

Denny hadn't been looking my way and, until then, was unaware of what had happened. He was just about to cross the fence, probably 30 yards off to my left, when he heard me start talking to the bird.

Once more, confronted with a fence that was just a bit too high to step over, I was trying to avoid being caught in an impossible situation if the bird flushed. I decided that the best course was to try to frighten the bird into taking wing, if it were still able to do so.

"Come on, bird, get up! Fly!" I encouraged the prostrate rooster, which was only a few paces beyond the fence.

Finally, my efforts were rewarded. The bird struggled to its feet, looked at me, and took a couple of steps in the opposite direction, as if badly intoxicated. Then it flapped its wings in an abortive takeoff attempt, briefly touched its landing gear to the ground again, and finally succeeded in getting itself airborne. I saluted the bird's departure with two misses.

Denny, who had heard me talking to the bird and who saw me miss, came over for an explanation. Initially, all I could do was shake my head in amazement. Then we both had a good laugh about how that bird had made a double escape—first from his encounter with the fence, and second from my off-target shots.

That incident took place over ten years ago. Denny still reminds me of it every time we hunt together. In the decade since then, I can't recall having talked any more roosters into flying.

Dave Prine and his chocolate Lab, Hoss, provided an interesting experience for me on a hunt in Mahaska County. Working some very dense grass cover, Hoss dove into the weeds and came out with a rooster in his mouth.

"Dog got a cripple?" I called to Dave, as he took the bird from Hoss.

"No, there's nothing wrong with this bird," said Dave, catapulting it into the air. I was stunned for a second, but recovered quickly enough to drop the departing bird.

Dave, who shoots live pigeons from time to time, had a big grin on his face. "Bet I'm the only columbaire who's ever thrown a pheasant," he joked.

My notes from the 1989 season reveal a couple of strange incidents from two separate hunts with Ed Wilson along a creek in northern Iowa. On both occasions, Heidi was directly involved.

The creek ran through a weedy field which was quite clearly a marsh in wet years. However, this was a relatively dry year, and there was no water anywhere except in the stream. The creek itself was too wide and too deep to cross and on our first hunt was not yet frozen solid.

We'd just come through a patch of especially heavy cover, weeds about waste high, and Heidi was definitely working birds. She seemed to be a little confused, probably an indication that more than one bird was running. She circled around in a patch of lighter cover, trying to pick up the trail.

Just then, a rooster went out low to my extreme left. The bird folded, and I hustled to the spot, afraid it might have dropped into the denser cover on the far side of the creek.

When I got to the bank, I spotted the bird on the thin ice, just short of the far bank. It was lying on its side, motionless, with only the wind ruffling its feathers.

Heidi finally spotted it as well, and I ordered her across to retrieve. She stepped gingerly onto the ice and made it about halfway across before she broke through. She struggled for half a minute or so, the ice breaking every time she tried to pull herself up. I was about ready to go in after her when she managed to extricate herself.

She wasn't very interested in testing the ice in another spot, and I obviously wasn't either. I was about to go on down the creek on our side, figuring I could cross the bridge on the road a quarter of a mile farther on, then come back on the opposite side for the bird.

About that time, my "dead" bird came to life. He stood up, eying me suspiciously for several seconds. I was pretty close for a shot, and I turned to Heidi, hoping that the sight of the cripple would send her on another attempt to cross the creek.

As I urged her across, I saw the pheasant hop up into the weeds on the other side. I fired, which was all the encouragement Heidi needed. She scooted across the creek, ahead of the cracking ice, hot after the bird. He came racing out of the cover and back onto the ice about 10 yards farther down, where I ended his career once and for all. This time, Heidi found a spot where she was, able to make the retrieve without breaking through.

A week or so later, we were hunting the same area again, within a few hundred yards of where that "dead" bird had nearly made his getaway. Heidi was working extremely thick marsh grass, so high that the only way I could keep track of her was the sound of the bell with which I always equip my dogs.

Then the bell stopped. Even though Heidi was well within gunshot, it took Ed and me some time to find her in the cover. When we did, she was frozen on point.

I walked in ahead of her, ready for the flush. I kicked the heavy marsh grass, expecting a pheasant to burst from in front of her nose. Instead, I was greeted with a growl from the tangle of vegetation.

I recoiled, as did Heidi. A raccoon lumbered out of its hiding place, clearly upset that we'd disturbed it. Fortunately, Heidi is not aggressive and simply moved aside to let the critter go on about its business. So did I.

Just as it is likely that you will encounter odd-acting birds— that raccoon had me momentarily convinced that I'd found a rooster that could growl—you will almost certainly run across odd-looking birds. The pheasant in America is such a hybrid that this should come as no real surprise.

However, there is an even more common reason for birds that don't quite look right. The fact that pheasant broods in the same area will hatch several weeks apart—often as much as a couple of months—makes for some big differences in appearance, especially early in the season.

On opening weekend several years ago, Gene Kroupa shot the smallest rooster I have ever seen bagged. Only the red patches around the bird's eyes gave it away. Gene told me that if the bird hadn't flown past him at close range, he never would have known it was a cock.

The more I hunt pheasants, the more convinced I am that some roosters make it through opening weekend because they can't be distinguished from hens. In 1989, my opening day party accounted for two tailless roosters that might well have survived had it not been a bright, sunny day. A week later, Mike Carroll and I let a bird reach extreme range before we fired, because until he let out a juvenile half-cackle, we mistook him for a hen.

My notebook and a photo I took remind me of a particularly odd-looking bird I shot several years ago. It was December, by which time even young roosters have full feathers and long tails, unless they've been shot off.

As we hunted four abreast through a wide strip of weeds leading up to a field of picked corn, a bird flushed from left to right in front of us. I was on the extreme right side of our line.

Mike Carroll, to my immediate left, fired as the bird crossed in front of him. He pulled tailfeathers, and I finished the bird off.

When I spotted Reb coming in with the bird in her mouth, I started to berate Mike. It looked for all the world like a hen, I told him, and I wouldn't have shot if he hadn't fired first.

"I'm sure that bird's a rooster," said Mike. All I could see were tan feathers, and I wasn't so sure. However, upon closer examination, I determined that Mike was right. The bird had a dark head, dark breast feathers, and a fully developed pair of spurs. DNR biologists later told me that the bird was simply a fluke. Occasionally, pheasants—like their close relative, the domestic chicken—produce individuals with characteristics of both sexes, like the hen that crows in the barnyard. But in all the years I've hunted, that's the only late-season, fully grown bird I've ever seen that looked almost more like a hen than a rooster.

It is amazing that roosters resemble one another as much as they do, when you consider all the strains of pheasants that have been imported. I have seen several true albinos mounted, although I wonder how many of them were wild birds. Some shooting preserves offer albino pheasants as a novelty. I have only encountered one in the wild, but I've spoken to many other experienced hunters who say that they've also seen white pheasants.

Other than the albino and the half-hen–half-rooster I just described, the oddest wild bird I've ever seen was one that I was lucky enough to kill. Unfortunately, the bird didn't drop dead, and Jake, who had had too many roosters peck him, spur him, and flap him in the face, got a bit rough with him. The dog didn't really mangle the bird, but it was not a good specimen for the taxidermist.

This particular rooster looked relatively normal except for its wings, which were white, and its head, which was white with black spots. I shot it near the little town of Clarksville, Iowa, and there were no shooting preserves or game farms anywhere in the vicinity. Although that is not an area where I've hunted a lot, I did see the albino bird less than 10 miles from there. Other people who hunt that area more than I do tell me that it seems to have more than its share of odd-looking birds.

Certainly, in their actions if not in their appearance, a few pheasants seem to stand out from among the many I encounter every season. To me, that is just another of the many charms of the sport.

Mixed Bag

HIS chapter covers a multitude of sins—topics which, although of importance to the pheasant hunter, don't really seem to rate treatment in a separate chapter and don't seem to fit neatly into other places in this book.

Since this is a "mixed bag" chapter, that topic seems to be a good place to start.

MIXED BAG HUNTS

Throughout much of its range, the pheasant is found in close company with other upland birds. In fact, some bird hunters actually seek out those situations where they are going to be surprised by what materializes when they step in front of their pointing dog or by what their Lab or spaniel causes to erupt from the brush.

Most of my experience comes in dealing with pheasant/quail hunts. This kind of mixed bag shooting is fairly common throughout the Midwest, especially in parts of Iowa, Kansas, and Nebraska. In Iowa, mixed bag hunting has become the rule rather than the exception in the southern third of the state, where you'll find the bulk of the bobwhite population. That situation has changed from fifteen years ago, when there were large chunks of southern Iowa with virtually no pheasants. Since then, the pheasant range has slid south, and the two birds seem to cohabitate very nicely.

Pheasants are often hunted together with other birds. One of the most popular mixed bag hunts is for pheasants and quail.

Although quail purists will shudder at the thought, I know a lot of midwestern hunters who do just fine gunning bobwhites in front of Labs or other flush dogs. It may not be classic gunning, but it produces results. Fellow Iowan Dave Prine claims that he actually prefers shooting quail, even though he bags probably twice as many pheasants in a normal season in front of his two Labs. When we get into bobwhites over my pointing dogs, he really enjoys himself.

The difficulty with a pheasant/quail mixed bag shoot is choosing guns and ammo. On those rare occasions when I'm in an area that has only bobwhites, my choice is likely to be a 28 gauge Hatfield with skeet/skeet barrels and Federal's Premium shells loaded with copper 8s. That combination is deadly on quail but only works on ringnecks if the birds are taken out to about 30 yards. I don't like to impose that kind of restriction on myself when shooting pheasants.

Prine, who is purely a 12 gauge shooter, uses custom-loaded

7s on both pheasants and quail. I have a 20 gauge SKB with choke tubes, which makes a pretty good mixed bag gun. Fitted with open chokes and using Winchester XX 2¾-inch magnum shells with 1⅛ ounces of 7½s, I'm about as well prepared for the ringneck/bobwhite combo as I can be.

Fumbling for shells or trying to guess which bird you're going to flush first has frustrated me on many occasions. In quail country, I used to pack both high-brass 6s and 1-ounce loads of 8s for my Sauer 16. I tried loading an 8 in the right barrel and a 6 in the left, or switching shells, depending on what we moved. It didn't work.

On one memorable occasion, Mike Carroll and I were loading up to assault a piece of public land near Rathbun Reservoir in southern Iowa. From the road, I spotted a number of pheasants as they sailed into a grassy draw about a quarter of a mile away. We both dropped in 6s and went after them.

Deke, my old Brittany, was doing the point-move–point-move maneuver so typical of a dog working running pheasants. I was watching him intently, waiting for him to lock up, when I stepped right in the middle of a covey of quail. With the impression only flushing quail can give, I thought that I must have disturbed a nest of giant feathered hornets. Birds seemed to be buzzing out everywhere.

I tried to pick out a single but hit only air. Mike, never a slow man on the trigger, got off two quick shots with his Winchester 101 20 gauge. The second resulted in a big puff of feathers. Deke broke off his search for pheasants to make the retrieve. The biggest piece he could find was a wing. That heavy load of 6s from a full-choke barrel at under 20 yards literally blew that bird away. Meanwhile, the pheasants were flushing to safety out the far end of the draw.

On another occasion, I was hunting solo with Jake in southeast Iowa, where my experience told me that I was much more likely to find pheasants than quail. We were working a strip of woods beside a picked soybean field. Jake slammed on point without warning at the edge of a dense patch of multiflora rose. That type of cover, and Jake's lack of "birdy" warning before he locked up, made me guess quail rather than pheasant. When the rooster flushed, I blew an easy chance on the first barrel. Fortunately, I recovered my composure and dumped him on the second shot.

I broke the Sauer, congratulated myself, and waited for Jake to go out and retrieve the cock from the nearly bare bean field, where it had fallen. Instead, Jake stiffened on point next to a tiny strip of foxtail, isolated in the middle of the otherwise bare ground. That piece of cover was maybe 2 feet wide by 10 feet long—an island in a picked soybean lake. The rooster was on the far side of the strip, and I assumed that Jake was simply making a point "dead."

I began to get suspicious when he refused to fetch at my command. I took a step forward and began to pluck the two empty hulls from the gun. As I did so, about fifteen quail rose in unison from the tiny strip. All I could do was stand and watch with an empty gun. I had dropped that rooster, which flushed from perfect bobwhite cover, about 5 yards from a covey which was hiding where no one would have expected.

And that may be the motto of the mixed bag hunt—expect the unexpected.

If you are going to a mixed bag area, try to match your gun and load to the situation. On a pheasant/quail expedition, you're going to want a relatively open choke, such as improved cylinder or improved cylinder/modified in a double. Heavy loads of 7½s are a good compromise.

When caught unprepared in such a situation, you can still adjust. If your gun is tightly choked, wait a bit longer on quail shots. If you have to choose between heavy 6s and light 8s, go with the 6s. They are not the best choice for quail, but they will do the job, especially from tighter chokes and at somewhat longer ranges. Carry a few 8s in case you break a covey and go after the singles. Don't expect that load to give you consistent performance on roosters.

Fortunately for the pheasant hunter, other birds often shot along with pheasants present less of a problem. Hungarian partridge and sharptail grouse are often taken on mixed bag hunts, but pheasant loads are good choices for both of these species.

Of course, there are oddball situations for which solutions are difficult. On a late October woodcock hunt along the Missouri River in southwest Iowa, I found pheasants and timberdoodles living in very close proximity. The woodcock hung out where the willows were thick enough that not much grass had grown up. Out toward the edge of the cover, where the trees were spaced out more and the grass thicker, the roosters were hiding. Although Jake nearly abandoned me because I refused to shoot the pheasants he pointed, I had no problem—the season opener was a week away. Had I returned the following weekend and had the woodcock still been in residence, I'm not sure how I would have handled that combination.

CLOTHING

Very few pheasant hunters give more than passing thought to what they wear afield. I have no quarrel with this attitude, as long as their clothing keeps them comfortable (meaning dry enough and either warm or cool enough, depending on the conditions) and does not hinder their shooting.

My dad used to shoot pheasants in bib overalls, in cold weather adding a hip-length denim jacket known among farmers as a "chore coat." Dad spent part of his youth on a farm, and he knew the utility of typical farmer garb. I think he also knew that he stood a better chance of getting permission to hunt private land if he didn't look like a city slicker.

Many Iowa farmers are rabid fans of either the University of Iowa Hawkeyes or the Iowa State Cyclones. They may sport emblems on their mailboxes, or even their barns. I spent several semesters as a part-time graduate student at Iowa and have taught at Iowa State, making me conveniently neutral. I carry caps from both institutions and choose the appropriate one, depending on the loyalties of the landowner with whom I'm negotiating for hunting rights.

But let's deal with the more functional purpose of clothing which I addressed initially—keeping you comfortable and not hindering your shooting. Let's start from the bottom up and get dressed for the hunt.

Boots may well be the most critical item of clothing. Tom Huggler nearly ruined a South Dakota pheasant hunt by using it to break in a new pair of boots which didn't quite fit right—blister city! If you're going to buy new boots, do so before the season, make sure they fit, and break them in.

I do nearly all my pheasant hunting in two pairs of boots. One is the old standby, L. L. Bean's Maine Hunting Shoe. This is the boot with the rubber bottom and leather upper. They are rugged, lightweight, and will keep your feet dry in all but the wettest weather. They are not the best choice for subzero hunting in the uninsulated version, and your feet will sweat some in them on very warm days. They do very well the rest of the time.

My newer selection is a pair of Gore-Tex Rocky Boots. Like

the Beans, they are light and waterproof. Your feet won't get as hot in them on warm days, and I prefer them when hunting in dry conditions. They saw a lot of use during the drought season of 1988. Despite their resistance to water, I go with the Beans on damp days. The Vibram soles on the Rocky boots quickly collect a couple of pounds of mud when you have to cross plowed fields or picked corn.

For extremely wet weather, I have a pair of uninsulated rubber boots. For Arctic cold, I use insulated leather boots. Both may see about one day of use per season. If it's that cold or that wet, I usually stay home and write about pheasant hunting.

All my boots are big enough so that I can wear two pairs of socks, usually a light pair of cotton athletic socks and a heavier pair of wool socks over them. At least in the Rocky boots, I've found that with this combination of socks, I don't have too much trouble with sweaty feet, even on very warm days.

I've never taken to bib overalls like my dad, although Dave Prine usually hunts ringnecks in a pair of Carhart bibs. They are made especially for hunting and are just about impossible to destroy.

My own preference runs to hunting pants faced with Cordura or, more recently, a pair of Cordura chaps over just about any old and comfortable trousers I happen to choose. The chaps are not waterproof, but even when I walk in soaking wet weeds, they do a pretty fair job of keeping me dry. I think part of the reason is the air space between the chaps and the trousers underneath. For the same reason, this arrangement keeps my legs pretty warm in all but the coldest weather, yet isn't terribly hot on warm, early-season outings.

Pheasant hunters may not spend as much time in the kind of cover that can rip your skin as do grouse and woodcock gunners, but there are times—like when you encounter multiflora rose or briars—that the extra layer of Cordura literally saves your skin.

I wear a hunting shirt without a jacket in almost all kinds of weather. I buy good quality chamois shirts, most often from L. L. Bean, a half size larger than normal. It isn't so bulky that it bothers my shooting, especially since I have a vest on anyhow. But it is large enough to allow me to slip a hooded sweatshirt under it on cold days.

I am probably a bad example of how to dress for cold-weather hunting. I've never hunted with anyone who wears less than I do in the winter. There have been plenty of seasons when I've never dug out my long underwear bottoms, nor worn anymore topside than a cotton T-shirt, hooded sweatshirt, chamois cloth shirt, and vest. That keeps me warm down pretty close to zero, depending, of course, on the wind.

I find that I have virtually no problem keeping warm as long as I'm moving. But each person has to adjust to his or her own individual thermostat.

I prefer a vest to a hunting coat because I don't need the extra warmth and bulk, and because I think that a vest allows me much greater freedom of arm movement. If you do a lot of bird hunting, I feel that a good vest or coat, like a good pair of boots, is well worth the investment.

I have several requirements for a pheasant hunting vest. First, it needs to be blaze orange. I think that there should be a blaze orange requirement for bird hunting, just as there is for many other types of hunting. Next, a pheasant vest has to have a game pouch which is big enough to hold three roosters. Those of you in Kansas might say four, with your generous limit, but I'm not sure anyone makes a pouch that big.

I think that a dozen shell loops are probably sufficient, although it doesn't hurt to have more. You shouldn't shoot up half a box of shells to get a limit of ringnecks, but you may need those extras if you're in mixed bag country. Finally, the shell loops should be protected by the flaps to your pockets. Exposed loops, in my estimation, do not belong on a vest or coat which is going to be worn through the briars and weeds. Before long, you'll have shredded loops, and you'll start to lose shells. My vest is Bob Allen's "Wing n' Shot" model, and I've been wearing it for a lot of years now. Not only does it fit all my requirements, but it seems to be impervious to such things as briars and barbed wire as well.

Caps and gloves are two accessories to which many pheasant hunters give little thought. In cold weather, they are absolutely critical, because body heat dissipates quickly through a bare head or hands. If you do feel that you are overheating, temporarily removing gloves or cap will usually get your thermostat back to the proper setting.

I wear a variety of caps, depending upon the weather. The opener usually finds me in a mesh baseball cap, which I exchange for a corduroy one as it turns colder. In the winter, I usually opt for a blaze orange Jones-style cap with a flannel lining. If it's really frigid, I may go to a heavy stocking cap. However, the hooded sweatshirt that I nearly always wear in cold weather gives me the option of slipping the hood up over the cap, thus eliminating the need for extremely warm headgear.

I'd probably wear the Jones cap in the early season if it were a bit cooler. It has just enough visor to shade my eyes, but not so much that it is likely to mess up my gun mounting. The baseball caps, on the other hand, can interfere with my shooting if I pull them down too far, in which case the long bill gets into my field of vision when I mount my gun.

I don't care much for gloves, especially on my trigger hand. I much prefer being able to feel the trigger and being able to operate the safety without a heavy layer between my skin and the metal.

For several years, I hunted with a tight glove on my left hand only—usually a baseball batting glove—to protect the bluing on my old Sauer, which has the smallest of splinter forearms, from too much contact with a sweaty hand. Recently I've switched to a very light pair of skeet gloves with Velcro fasteners. I like them even better than no gloves at all, because they keep me from fumbling around with the safety or the trigger if my hands do sweat.

Unfortunately, they offer little protection from the cold. With temperatures down into the teens, I use jersey gloves, which have the palms and fingers covered with little dots. They are not bulky, provide positive gripping, and cost about two dollars per pair. The only problem is that they are worthless if they get wet. But because they are so cheap, I usually carry a spare pair in my hunting bag to use while I'm drying the wet ones with the pickup heater.

Steve Grooms and I once made the mistake of chasing pheasants in −50 degree windchill. On that particular hunt, the only gloves I could find which would keep my hands warm enough and still allow me to shoot were a pair of insulated buckskin gloves. They also have a cuff which fits snugly around the wrist, keeping snow from getting inside and cold from sneaking in between glove and shirtsleeve.

Finding acceptable heavy gloves may be a particular problem for hunters with some double-trigger guns. If the trigger guard is too small, a bulky glove may make it impossible for you to get your finger between it and the first trigger, or between the two to fire the second barrel. Fortunately, my old Sauer has plenty of room. If your gun looks like it might be a tight fit, try out the gloves before you wear them hunting and make the assumption that they'll work.

On that same −50 degree hunt, I also wore a ski mask and an Army field jacket over about three layers of shirts. We actually killed a few birds that day, but not enough to make it worth the effort. There is a difference between uncomfortable and miserable, and we crossed the line on that day. I'll hunt uncomfortable if I think that there is a good chance of getting some shots, but I have reached the point where nothing is worth miserable.

One other item of clothing which proved of great value to me during the 1985 season, when we had a lot of snow, is a pair of gaiters like those worn by cross-country skiers. When hunting in deep, fluffy snow without gaiters, your options are both losers: tuck your pants in, and the snow will eventually sift down inside your boots; leave them out, and snow will get up inside, chilling your legs. Gaiters are waterproof, not bulky, and will keep the snow both out of your boots and off your legs. Hunting in deep snow is uncomfortable enough without worrying about wet feet or cold legs.

MAPS

Although much has been said about the value of maps in such sports as deer and turkey hunting, and even in locating grouse and woodcock coverts, no one talks much about maps for the pheasant hunter. While the topographic maps favored by those who hunt game in more remote parts of the country are of little use to the pheasant hunter, I am a strong believer in the value of other types of maps.

My hunting bag contains a booklet called the *Iowa County Map Guide*. This booklet, which cost five dollars when I bought it back in about 1986, is published by State and Local Publications, Inc. (527 Chapel Hill, Elkhorn, Nebraska 68022; telephone: [402] 289-3072). It has full-page maps of every county in the state, showing all secondary roads. The maps also have public hunting areas, state parks, recreational areas, etc., all color-coded for easy identification.

I find these maps useful for a couple of reasons. If I'm looking for a new public hunting area, the directions (4 miles east and 6 miles south of Haystack, Iowa) are often a bit difficult to follow without a map. Likewise, when you find a good farm to hunt, you can mark it on the appropriate page, make a note in the margin, and hopefully find it again when you want to return.

The information I have indicates that the same company

publishes similar guides for other states.

The other map I use a lot, particularly in those areas where I hunt often, is a county plat book. It is much more detailed, with one good general county map and each township of the county (about 36 square miles) shown on individual pages.

The plat books show property lines and give names of owners and tenants of each piece of land. Most also have alphabetical indexes, which will give you the phone number of that friendly farmer who invited you back and whom you'd like to call in advance, or perhaps afterwards, to convey your thanks.

Land ownership used to be pretty predictable, with your average farmer living on and farming the same piece of ground. Things have gotten much more complex, especially with the economic turmoil which befell farmers in the Midwest in the 1980s. A farmer may own a small piece of ground where he or she lives but may not farm anything within a couple of miles of the house. Or the farmer may own, rent, or lease. These may well be some distance from the "home place."

A plat book will give you a much more accurate idea of what farmers are talking about when they say something like, "I've got another quarter section you can hunt, too—couple of miles north, then a mile west, then half a mile north." I'm always a bit leery of getting all of that straight, at which point I whip out my plat book. Most farmers are impressed if you show that you are so concerned about knowing where you can and can't hunt that you carry a plat book.

Be aware that ownership and lease agreements change fairly frequently. Always check with the farmer to see if that 80 with the creek running through it 3 miles down the road is still in his or her possession.

Plat books cost around five dollars and are usually sold by the county recorder at the courthouse. If you hunt one particular county much, it's a good idea to get a new plat book every three or four years in order to keep up with changes in boundaries and land ownership.

SPARES

No, this section will not deal with carrying an extra tire for your vehicle, although that is one spare you shouldn't ignore on a hunting trip. What I am going to discuss here are items of spare gear which are a bit more closely related to a pheasant hunter's specific needs.

When I first started carrying spares, everything that I thought I might need fit into a battered old gym bag. About all I carried were some extra shells, a change of socks, and perhaps a heavier or lighter shirt.

These days, I don't venture out without a fairly substantial duffel bag—the kind with a full-length zipper—just about stuffed full. In addition, the back of my pickup has a couple of wooden boxes as permanent equipment. Although one contains items for the truck itself, the other is filled with what amounts to overflow from my hunting bag.

And that's only for a one-day trip. If I venture farther from home, my pickup starts sagging from the load.

Here is a list of items, by categories, that I feel are necessary spares for a pheasant hunter:

1. *Clothing.* I now carry a full set, from underwear on out, even on a one-day hunt. It stays permanently stashed in one of my wooden truck boxes, because it's also handy on fishing trips in the off season. Hunt long enough on a rainy day and you'll learn the value of dry clothes. Or step off a creekbank into knee-deep water and land on your rear instead of your feet, as I did once when encouraging Jake to retrieve a rooster across a steeply sided stream.

Although, as mentioned earlier, I believe strongly in a couple pair of good boots, there is no need for extravagance in the spare clothes department. An old pair of combat boots nestle in with my change of clothing. While I wouldn't normally wear them hunting, they work fine in a pinch for a couple of hours and are far preferable to hunting in soaked boots, or quitting, or driving home 50 miles to get another pair.

I think that it is especially important to carry a variety of caps and gloves. I've seen it go from 20 degrees to 60 degrees, or vice versa, in the course of a one-day hunt. It's nice to be able to change to cooler or warmer head and hand wear.

2. *Shells.* This is especially important for those oddballs like me who hunt with a 16 gauge. Ever try to find 16s at the local Gas & Go? Or borrow them from your partners, all of whom shoot 12s and 20s? My gun case has a little zipper pocket that will hold about half a box of shells. I usually put half a dozen extra pheasant loads and half a dozen quail loads in there. In addition,

Larry Brown is a strong believer in that old Boy Scout motto, "Be prepared." About to depart on a long hunting trip, you see him with two dogs, an extra gun, and a bag full of other necessary spares.

I'll usually carry at least part of another box somewhere in the bottom of my duffel bag.

3. Maps. This category includes a good road map of the state I'm hunting and the county maps and plat books mentioned earlier. I stuff mine in a heavy nylon bag which I believe used to hold a tent fly. In addition to the maps, the same bag has room for a brochure listing public hunting areas, a copy of the hunting laws, and my notebook, along with a couple of pens or pencils.

4. Miscellaneous hunting gear. Whatever I wear while hunting but not while riding goes into the bag. This usually includes a hunting vest, chaps, and a cheap, idiot-proof 35-mm camera for taking pictures in the field.

5. *Miscellaneous dog gear.* At a minimum, I'll carry an extra bell, whistle, collar, and leash. If one of my canine companions needs a bit of a refresher course afield, I'll also include my electronic collar and transmitter.

Now for a couple of somewhat more controversial items, ones which you do not necessarily need to include on a one-day hunt, but which I have found to be essential to the success of a hardcore pheasant hunter.

The first is an extra gun. You say that you can always buy one if worse comes to worst? Not with our current gun laws, if you happen to be hunting out of state. Also, think about getting used to that new gun. Unless you find an exact replacement for your old gun, you may frustrate yourself for most of the season.

Here I speak from experience. In 1980 my Sauer took ill on a woodcock hunt and wasn't out of the hospital until after the end of pheasant season. I had an extra gun—nothing fancy, mind you, just a little Kasnar over-and-under 20, double triggers, light and fast handling. I'd popped a couple of rounds of skeet with the gun when I first got it, then relegated it to the closet until needed.

The Kasnar got its call for opening day of grouse season. That just happened to be the best year for ruffed grouse I've ever seen in Iowa, before or since. I had fourteen shots, many of them easy. As far as I could tell, I didn't touch a feather. Only cooler heads in the hunting party kept me from wrapping that little Italian superposed around a tree.

I finally discovered the problem. The gun simply didn't fit. I could hit with it, calling for the birds with the gun shouldered, as I had at skeet. But when I brought it up on the spur of the moment, as in to deal with a flushing grouse or pheasant, it wasn't even close to being on. I sold it to a guy about a foot taller than me, who told me that it fit him just fine. We were both happy.

With the proceeds from that sale, plus a bit of additional cash, I bought a BSS Sporter—26-inch 20 gauge double, straight stock, choked improved cylinder and modified. Before I took it to South Dakota after October pheasants, I used it on a few unfortunate Iowa woodcock. We seemed to be a good team.

However, Iowa woodcock were not Dakota ringnecks coming over the top of a shelterbelt like driven birds in Great Britain. Maybe I wouldn't have hit many of them anyhow, but I sorely missed either the Sauer's longer barrels or else the slightly heavier 16 gauge loads, or perhaps both. I swore never to get caught without a totally reliable backup gun again.

The next time the Sauer failed me was in the middle of November 1985. This time, I switched to an old Ithaca 16 gauge field grade with which I had taken the time to become familiar. From then until the end of the season, I went twenty-one for forty-two with my spare gun, which although nothing to write home about, was actually better than I'd shot with the Sauer before it broke.

The beauty of requiring a spare gun, of course, is that you can justify spending some extra bucks on hunting gear and some off-season hours prowling sporting goods shops and gun shows. What you spend is up to you. I would advise, however, that your spare gun be similar to what you're used to, or that you take the time to become adequately acquainted with it. For instance, if you're a pump gunner, I wouldn't advise an autoloader as a backup. You may jerk off the magazine trying to get the slide to work.

Although the stock fit on my two 16s was a bit different, they were both double-trigger side-by-sides. I also used the Ithaca quite a bit on grouse, woodcock, and preserve birds and at skeet. That helped a lot.

Most of my hunting career, I haven't been able to afford any more than one good shotgun. When I've had two, it seems that I've always felt that owning the second one wasn't justified because it sat around and gathered dust most of the time. I've parted with several nice backup guns. Of course, now that I have a couple which would serve quite nicely, the old Sauer works like a charm.

Don't let me convince you to break the family budget. As long as it works and you can shoot it, your backup gun doesn't have to be anything fancy. Chances are that if you have something a bit more normal than my Sauer as your primary armament, it won't spend much time in the shop, anyhow. But be ready if it does.

The serious pheasant hunter should also consider the wisdom of owning a "spare" dog. I've found that hunting dogs are even a bit more fragile than shotguns. Unlike a gun, their life expectancy can be extended just so far, even given the best of care.

Those who get out only once a weekend or so during the season and who do little additional hunting probably cannot justify owning two dogs in their prime. That kind of a schedule doesn't really provide enough work to keep more than one canine in top form. However, if you have only one dog, another of

Brown's laws states that your four-footed partner is almost certain to be afflicted with something during the course of the season, leaving you dogless for a certain period of time.

The following brief chronology of my dogs' ailments should clearly illustrate why I think that it's a good idea to have a couple of dogs available:

1981—Jake developed an abscess on his side, which eventually grew to the size of a grapefruit. The vet drained it and sewed him back up. He missed the first half of December, until the stitches were removed.

1983—Jake had a particularly persistent bout with hookworms in the fall. Although he was clean of parasites by the opening day of pheasant season, I did not realize that it had left him severely anemic.

After about an hour and a half chasing birds in frost-covered weeds, Jake simply stopped hunting. He was cold and wet, but that had never bothered him much, especially when the air temperature was in the mid-30s. I took him to the local vet, who explained that what Jake had in effect was hypothermia. A quick check of his gums showed that they were pale instead of a healthy pink—anemia from the bout with worms.

For most of the remainder of that season, Jake could hunt for only about two hours at a stretch. I had to be particularly careful on cold or wet days, drying him with a towel or blanket and allowing him to warm up in the truck. I also carried a tube of concentrated, high-energy food supplement called Nutri-Cal, which I fed to him to help keep him going.

1984 and 1985—Like 1982, these were unusual in that they were seasons when I didn't have anything more than barbed wire scrapes or bloody tails to contend with. By the start of the 1985 season, Rebel was a year and a half old and ready to carry more of a load to spell her hard-going father.

1986—Two weeks into the season, Jake went down with severe hindquarter problems. I had discovered that he had hip dysplasia a couple of years earlier, when a kennel owner who wanted to breed Jake to his bitch had him X-rayed at Iowa State University. The litter that produced Rebel was already born by then, and I had her spayed out of concern that she might pass on the dysplasia.

However, Jake didn't hunt like a dysplastic dog. With the exception of a few instances when he would turn up stiff in the morning after two or three hard days in a row, nothing seemed to slow him down. Dysplasia has different effects on different dogs, and because Jake was already well into middle age, I had every reason to expect that he would give me several more good years afield.

I was surprised by the suddenness of the 1986 episode. Jake had been hunting very well for the first part of the season. We were working a couple of acres of waste ground between two cornfields when a rooster got nervous and offered me a particularly long chance. I took it and folded the bird. As usual, Jake marked the fall and needed no encouragement to retrieve.

When he didn't return as quickly as I thought he should, I put it down to a long retrieve and the possibility of a running bird. Finally, I saw Jake struggle up a deep ditch separating the patch I was hunting from the corn, rooster in his mouth. I ran forward to praise him. It was then I discovered that his hindquarters were almost nonfunctional. We immediately headed back to the truck, Jake having difficulty keeping up even though I walked slowly.

When I took Jake to the vet, he felt, as I did, that it was simply the dysplasia catching up with him. I hunted Jake a few more times over the next month, with plenty of rest in between, and he did recover enough to function for hunts of an hour or so if he had a day or two to rest in between.

Then, on the morning of December 14, I found Jake dead in his kennel. Because he hadn't seemed to be ill other than the hindquarter problem, and because he'd been eating relatively well, I was stunned by the suddenness of his death. Fearing something contagious, I had the vet do an autopsy. The verdict was a nonfunctioning heart valve, which, rather than the dysplasia, almost certainly caused what happened in the field when he came up lame. The vet assured me that there was nothing that could have been done even had we known.

It is always hard to lose a dog, more so when one means as much to you as Jake did to me. He was the first really good pheasant dog I ever owned. The only consolation was that some of him lived on in his daughter Rebel, who picked up the hunting chores for the remainder of the season.

Having acquired Rebel as a pup while Jake was still in his prime, I had had the luxury of bringing her along slowly. The previous season, 1985, she had done pretty well for a youngster—twenty-one productive points in twenty-seven hours of hunting. During the latter part of the 1986 season, after Jake's death, she came on like a champ. She made forty-four points in fifty-seven hours of hunting, and I killed a total of twenty birds over her. Even with Jake gone, I looked forward to 1987 with anticipation.

1987—This was supposed to be Rebel's year. Instead, I nearly lost her to a severe kidney infection in September. Although she recovered, she was still in a somewhat run-down state by the time pheasant season opened. She was to have been my number one dog, with Heidi, her new kennel-mate, spelling her as needed. The roles ended up being reversed.

The positive side of Rebel's health problems was that I'd been forced to give Heidi a lot of work. Rebel wasn't even able to make the trip to Michigan for a week of woodcock and grouse shooting. Heidi did it solo, and although she had never seen a woodcock before she got there, she did a great job. Nineteen eighty-seven was an excellent pheasant season, and Heidi made nearly one hundred productive points before it was over. The forty-nine roosters I killed over her were more than I'd ever shot previously in an entire season—and I was also hunting Rebel when she was up to it.

1988—With Rebel back to full strength and Heidi coming off an incredible rookie season, my canine corps was in the best shape ever. Then Heidi developed an abscess behind her eye, requiring surgery and putting her out of action for the last half of November. Rebel was able to pick up the slack.

I don't think that my dog problems have been atypical. While pets may live far beyond the age of 10, hunting dogs often meet earlier and more tragic ends. Talk to anyone who has owned many bird dogs and you will find that a dog which has kept on hunting into his double digit years is the exception rather than the rule.

Even having two dogs does not guarantee you that one will always be ready to go. Pointers have a tendency to develop bloody tails from crashing through the brush. Both Jake and Rebel experienced this problem. Rebel had cut hers pretty badly on grouse and woodcock, and it hadn't totally healed when Jake died. Although I tried to protect it with gauze, tape, and various other coverings, I was mostly unsuccessful.

Eventually, I decided to wrap it and give her a few days to recover before hunting again. When I saw the bandage in her kennel run one morning, I thought that she'd managed to defeat my efforts again. Closer inspection revealed that she'd sloughed off the injured tip of her tail, which is now 4 inches shorter than it used to be. She never did have the classic long pointer tail like her father, and were she not so petite and so clearly all English pointer, skeptics might almost believe her to be a long-tailed shorthair.

I think that I've made my point. But as I said earlier, the casual hunter really can't justify owning more than one adult dog. For those in that category, I'd suggest acquiring a pup about the time your adult dog is entering the twilight of its career—say, somewhere around the age of 7 or 8, depending on its condition. That way, if things work out as they should, your pup can come along slowly while the old-timer carries the brunt of the hunting duties. And when the old dog is ready for retirement, the youngster will be groomed for its slot in the starting lineup.

In my own case, however, and in that of most really hardcore pheasant chasers, there is ample reason to have a couple of fully trained canines in the kennel. I justify this procedure not only to keep me hunting in the event one of the dogs is laid up but also because, if both remain healthy, I probably hunt either one of them more than most hunters hunt only one dog.

I'll go entire seasons without hunting my two dogs together. In fact, if I'm only going out for a half-day hunt, I'll probably leave one at home. But on a typical all-day hunt, my tactic is to hunt one for a couple of hours, then the other, and finish the day with the first dog. This gives you an animal that is fully rested at all times. I also feel that it is easier on the dogs in the long run if you do not try to hunt one animal day in and day out for most of a two-month season. I doubt that I could hunt Rebel that much, because she simply has never learned to pace herself. Heidi could probably do it, but I'd rather spare her from that much work.

Another advantage of having two dogs is that, assuming they are of different breeds or different hunting styles, you can pick the dog that fits the situation. Heidi is excellent along narrow waterways and fencerows, which is where I do much of my hunting. Rebel is far too fast to be ideally suited to that kind of cover. But put her down in a set-aside field full of fence-to-fence cover and she's in her element. While I can use Heidi in a situation like that, it will take me considerably longer to cover the same piece of ground. Each of the two has her own niche.

Is it worth the expense to kennel, feed, and care for a second dog for whatever advantage it will give you during the all too brief months of the hunting season? It is to me. I believe that if you think it over, you will also come to the conclusion that two dogs are much more of a necessity than they are a luxury.

GETTING IN SHAPE

Now that I've discussed dogs and the frequent difficulties of keeping one of them in condition to make it through a long, hard season, I need to talk about the human half of the pheasant hunting team. It also has a tendency to break down from time to time, increasingly so with age. But a bit of prevention can keep much of this normal wear and tear from putting you out of action.

Pheasant hunting is not among the most strenuous of sports. While it may be tougher than sitting in a duck blind or riding a mule-drawn wagon after quail on a Southern plantation, it is easier than fighting your way through the thick stuff after grouse and woodcock. For the most part, the terrain is flat and open. In most places I've hunted, walking long distances with a gun would be a pretty fair description of the physical activity involved. Of course, there is the occasional creek to ford or jump, the occasional fence to scale, and such hindrances to optimum footing as snow or mud.

If you're not carrying too much weight, and if you don't have problems with your legs, you don't need to prepare for a pheasant hunt like you would for an assault on Mt. Everest. However, the cumulative effect of several successive days in the field can be a problem, especially for people who have sedentary jobs. My father, who hunted pheasants until he was almost 70, never had much of a problem. But he was also a factory worker who did hard physical labor. He didn't have to do anything to keep in shape except go to work. Most of us do not fall into that category.

If your cardiovascular fitness is good, and if you are capable of walking long distances, you can handle pheasant hunting. And if you hunt a lot, that in itself will take care of your exercise needs during the season.

In my own case, I've gotten into the habit of exercising on a year-round basis. I'm an officer in the Army Reserve, and we are required to take a physical fitness test once a year. The test consists of push-ups, sit-ups, and a 2-mile run. I usually ignore the push-ups, which I hate, and the sit-ups, which have always been fairly easy for me, until a month or so before I'm tested. But I run most of the year, except during hunting season.

There are all kinds of reasons not to run. Many people, myself included, find it somewhat boring. Some people claim it will lead to injury. My experience is that the majority of running injuries occur in two groups of people: the very good runners, who overexert to do their best in a race, or those who are out of shape and go at it too hard before their bodies are ready.

There are runners and there are *runners*. I belong to the first group. I'm no threat to win even age-group prizes in any races I enter, unless they are very small. In lightly attended medium-distance races, I do well if I finish ahead of all the women—not really a small feat anymore, because there are a lot of serious female runners. I'm happy if my best mile and 2-mile times are competitive with the top girl distance runners on the local high school track team. I figure that isn't bad for a guy in his mid-forties, and in fact it's nearly always good enough to beat just about all the soldiers, even those half my age, when we take our Army PT test.

Distance running is like shooting a shotgun. You can make significant improvement through practice. Do it enough and you may wish to enter a couple of races a year, or even go to the crazy extent I did in my first year of competitive running and try a marathon. I finished that 26-miler in roughly nine-minute miles. But every time I think that I want to do another one, I remember what the first one was like.

Racing, however, is unimportant. You certainly don't need to do it to be in excellent shape for pheasant hunting. The only thing it gets me, when one of my "buddies" brings it up to a new member of our hunting party, is another guy who is bound and determined to walk me into the ground. I'd rather enjoy myself on a pheasant hunt and save the racing for the off-season.

Experts say that about a half hour of good exercise three to four times a week is the requirement for cardiovascular conditioning. A half hour of running, regardless of the speed, will do it for you. A ten-minute mile will seem slow if you compare it to the world's record, but it's plenty fast for conditioning.

As a matter of fact, thirty minutes of solid running is almost certainly too much for someone who is not physically active. Even though I hunt quite frequently throughout the season, probably covering 20 miles a week as an average, I only start with 2 miles or so of running when I pick it up again in late winter.

When you start out, try alternating running with walking. Run five minutes, walk five minutes, run again, and so on, until you've exercised for thirty minutes. It may take you several weeks to build up to the point where you can run the entire half hour comfortably.

If you are overweight, a smoker, have a heart condition or a history of family heart problems, or if you're over 40, you should have a physical before you start any exercise program. And remember—don't push at the start.

The beauty of running is that you don't need much equipment except a decent pair of shoes, and they will last you for about 500 miles. But there are certainly other options. Some critics of running say that walking is just as good. This is partially true. You can get about as much benefit from walking 3 miles at a brisk pace as you can from running the same distance. The problem is that, even if you're a slow jogger, it's likely to take you nearly twice as long to walk a given distance. But running is not suitable for everyone, especially those with knee problems.

Biking is great, too, although you have to put a bit of effort into it to get results. The old saw about "no pain, no gain" is quite true in exercise. However, don't go to the other extreme. Too much pain during exercise won't get you in shape—it will just get you more pain, and you'll quit worse off than when you started.

Swimming is also a good cardiovascular exercise, but it does not do as much for the legs as any of the others I've mentioned.

While I'm addressing exercise here as a way of getting you through the hunting season comfortably, it has many benefits for your overall health. I have a resting pulse rate in the low 50s, cholesterol count well under 200, and blood pressure of around 100 over 80. That's partly due to the genes I inherited and partly to not smoking, but exercise is an important factor, especially in lowering pulse rate and cholesterol.

Exercise is also important in weight control but is often overemphasized. For example, if you do not modify your diet, you have to run about 30–40 miles to lose a pound! Exercise will move the weight around and will convert fat to muscle—but because muscle is heavier, your weight loss will not be great. A former gym teacher of mine, who was also a very successful wrestling coach, once advised push-ups for weight loss. When someone asked him to elaborate, he said, "You just have to push yourself away from the table."

Our society has a fixation on weight, and thin has been in for quite some time. While it can be carried to an extreme, most of us realize that we are carrying ten or twenty pounds that we don't really need. Getting rid of some or all of that prior to the hunting season will mean that much less you have to carry around in the field. Personally, if I'm going to carry extra pounds, I'd prefer it to be a limit of roosters in my hunting vest.

E T H I C S

I once heard ethics defined as the way you behave when you're by yourself and you're sure no one else will see you. I equate it to not speeding, even if there aren't any cops around.

Ethics are important in hunting because most of the time there is no one around to referee your behavior. Even if you do stay within the letter of the law, do you occasionally do things you wouldn't tell your buddies about? Maybe the temptation got too much for you and you ground-swatted a perfectly healthy rooster. Although that isn't illegal, at least not in most places I know of, it is the kind of behavior which most pheasant hunters would frown on. In other words, most of us agree that shooting pheasants on the ground is unethical.

Ethics will vary from person to person, and when selecting hunting partners, finding someone whose ethics are compatible with yours is very important. For example, many pheasant hunters practice what I call party shooting. In other words, if there are three of you hunting and the daily bag limit is three roosters, you multiply three times three and come out with a party limit of nine. It makes no difference whether you each shoot three, or whether one shoots five, another three, and the bad shot of the group only one. You still get your party limit.

Strictly speaking, party shooting is probably illegal in most places. However, it is not something with which you are likely to be charged by a game warden. You throw the birds in the back of the station wagon, and who is to know who shot how many?

The point is that you know, and if you are uncomfortable about it, you should make your feelings clear to the other members of the group. If I'm hunting with strangers, I let them know that I prefer to shoot my own birds and that I'm not so hard up for meat that I need someone else to shoot them for me. (There are, of course, those days when, either due to poor shooting or all of the birds flushing in front of the other guys, that the only way I'd get birds is with someone else's help. I'd rather go without, thank you.)

I'll admit to participating in party shooting on a few occasions. Once I was hunting with a farmer who wasn't a very good shot. He did get one bird, and I rationalized that he told me to shoot the other ones for him. Even though he was happy with "his" limit, I was not entirely happy with myself.

Of course, there are those gray areas which even the most stringent code of ethics cannot solve. I rarely hunt without one or the other of my own dogs, and in fact they are often doing the bird-finding for at least one other hunter. If I shoot my limit but the others are short of theirs, what do I do? Whistle up my dogs and say, "Sorry, guys, but that's it?"

I've had that happen often enough that I've come to a solution which fits my own code of ethics but which might not satisfy everyone else. I continue hunting as long as the rest of the party wishes to do so. My gun stays loaded, but I shoot only to finish a bird crippled by someone else, which might otherwise escape. My ethics tell me that it is more important to recover a cripple than it is for me to worry about whether I shoot one too many birds.

Ethics are not absolute like laws, and you are foolish if you think that everyone else will agree with your ethics. My own ethics are significantly different than my father's. He shot far more pheasants on the ground than he ever did in the air. I accept that in him, both because he taught me so many other valuable things about hunting and because he comes from a different era. I would not accept it from any of my hunting contemporaries.

There are some anglers, the so-called fly fishing purists, who will only take fish with flies. There are some bird hunters who will only shoot over points. That is their decision to make, and I respect them for it. They probably only feel comfortable hunting and fishing with people of like persuasions.

Personally, I think that is carrying ethics a bit too far. On the other hand, there are plenty of hunters who will say that anything legal is ethical. While I won't spend much time or effort trying to change their opinion, because I think that they have a right to it, I also won't spend any time hunting with them.

THE HUNTER'S NOTEBOOK

If you read enough about hunting, you will discover that hunters have been keeping records of their exploits afield for well over a century. In my own case, I have to give George Bird Evans credit for inspiring me to do so. I read his book, *The Upland Shooting Life,* while I was overseas. When I returned to Iowa in 1973, I started recording my hunts.

Like Evans, I've discovered that my notes have grown more detailed over the years. I started using the little 3-by-5-inch pocket notebooks and would often get two or three entries to a page. I've since graduated to the 6-by-9½-inch variety, and I will often fill a page with one day's hunt.

After listing the date, I try to record a brief synopsis of the day's hunt—location, number of birds moved, how many shots I took and how many I hit, points by my dogs. I'll also mention how I hunted the cover and how the birds reacted. I may add a note to myself concerning a better way to tackle the particular spot next time around. Then I conclude with the time of day and weather conditions—temperature, wind direction and velocity, cloud cover, and ground condition (dry, muddy, frozen, amount of snow, if any).

Rereading these notes can be a very educational experience. You will, of course, be able to evaluate your own shooting and your dog's work over one or more seasons. You may also pick up patterns of behavior by the birds under given conditions. But even if you don't learn anything—and you almost certainly will— the notebooks are an excellent way of jogging your memory about past hunts. I can go back to that very first diary, now nearly twenty years old, and remember those long-gone moments with Deke, and the frustrations of trying to get him to adapt to Iowa pheasants.

My notes are by no means great works of literature. They are the mere jottings of a tired hunter, usually written after the dogs have been cared for, the game dressed, and the gun cleaned—or perhaps scribbled down under a setting sun, right after the hunt has ended. Even though they form the basis of this book, in notebook form they are of value to no one but me. Yet to me they are priceless, because what they contain are memories of dogs who hunt no more, of places where the cover and the birds disappeared a decade ago, and of good times alone or with good companions afield. They are the best way I know to relive seasons past. And in that too-long interval which stretches from the end of one season to the beginning of the next, they help make the time pass more quickly.

Fee Hunting

ITH the exception of those who have experienced South Dakota pheasant hunting, most of us much past age 35 remember when fee hunting for pheasants was unheard of—it was all free for the asking. But as we head into the twenty-first century, some pheasant hunters wonder whether free hunting will indeed be replaced by fee hunting. In this chapter, we'll do a bit of crystal ball gazing in an attempt to answer that question, and we'll also examine the current state of fee hunting in its various guises.

As Americans, we may not realize how lucky we are to enjoy so much free hunting. This is not the case in Europe, and there are a couple of very good reasons why the situation there is different.

One of those reasons is historical. Before democracy took root on European soil, hunting rights were reserved for royalty and the nobility. Remember Robin Hood, who became an outlaw for poaching the king's deer? It wasn't just that poor Robin shot the wrong deer or did it in the wrong place. What he did was a crime anywhere in the land.

Although the story isn't widely accepted today, one of the legends surrounding the development of the Brittany as a gun dog is that it was used by peasants from the French province of the same name who poached game. In France, hunting by commoners was forbidden until after the revolution.

Today, pay hunting in Europe is still the rule, partly based on the historical exclusiveness of the sport. Also, because only the

Many people hunt pheasants on shooting preserves. This preserve rooster almost sat too tight for its own good.

nobility hunted for so many years, a tradition of hunting among the common folk never developed. Of all the nations of Europe, France has the greatest number of hunters, at about half a million. That's less than 1 percent of the total population. Here in America, something more like 10 percent of the population hunts.

The other problem in Europe is demographics. Population densities are extremely high in most countries. France, about the size of Texas, has a population of about sixty million, which

On a pre-season preserve trip, Heidi delivers a quail.
Preserve hunting is great for dog training and an
excellent way to extend the season.

means there are about four Frenchmen for every Texan. And France is one of the less densely populated countries by European standards, much less so than Belgium, Holland, or England.

In short, Europe has a lot of people, and most European nations simply do not have the relatively empty plains and forests we do. There isn't a lot of European land in the public domain, and very little of what does belong to the government is managed for hunting.

Of course, at the other end of the spectrum, Europe provides numerous examples of the best developed game management programs anywhere in the world. The epitome of this is almost certainly reflected in the driven grouse and pheasant shooting in Great Britain, where very high numbers of birds are produced on what would be small parcels of land by our standards.

But these shoots, of course, are the direct end product of

money—lots of it. Europe does not have a lot of hunters, but among those it does have number some very wealthy people, willing to pay what to us are unbelievable amounts of money for their sport.

Contrast all of this with our situation, where with our heritage of the wild frontier, which has really only been "tamed" for less than a century, hunting is something we have always had for free and taken for granted at that.

The first type of fee hunting to gain widespread acceptance in this country was the shooting preserve. On these establishments, obviously, hunting was looked upon as a business. The preserve owner provided goods—in most cases, feathered game of one species or another—for clients who were willing to pay for it.

Once strictly the province of the rich, much like European hunting in that respect, shooting preserves now have a much broader client base. In fact, the preserve business is booming in many parts of the country.

Where game is scarce or access to private and public hunting land difficult, this popularity is easy to understand. But many may ask why preserves are doing so well in parts of the country, such as the Midwest, where pheasant hunting is holding its own, if not improving, and where it is not all that hard to find a place to hunt.

There are a couple of answers to this question. One is that preserves are able to offer a much longer open season in nearly all states. In my home state of Iowa, which has a generously long 2½-month pheasant season, the preserve season is open from the beginning of September to the end of March.

The second is the service that the preserves provide. Older hunters, for example, may still have the physical capacity to shoot birds but not to walk the long distances often required in wild bird hunting. Likewise, at the other end of the age spectrum, hunters training their children may wish to do so in a setting where they know game will be found and interest will remain high.

Also, with more and more pheasant hunters owning dogs, preserves give an excellent opportunity for additional pre- and post-season training and polishing of one's canine companion.

And finally, the cost is well within what the market will bear. Preserve pheasants probably average out at between twelve to twenty dollars per bird released, which isn't all that bad when

you consider the time and effort you may put into shooting a two-
or three-bird limit chasing wild birds.

The major concern expressed by most hunters who have not
experienced preserve shooting, in addition to the very idea of
paying for one's birds, is how much of a challenge these "tame"
birds offer.

Having hunted three different preserves on several occasions, I can say with some authority that it isn't like shooting fish
in the proverbial barrel. All in all, while I find them easier than
wild birds, preserve pheasants pose enough challenge to main-
tain most hunters' interest.

Both of my dogs have been on numerous preserve hunts. I
take advantage of the excellent cover and the fact that the birds
often hold longer and tighter than their wild counterparts to do
photography work I seldom risk while "open hunting."

Dan Mullin, who runs Arrowhead Hunting Club in Clinton
County, Iowa, was assisting me with photos on one hunt. Reb
had a rooster nailed in the grass, and Dan maneuvered to get
some different angles as I walked in behind the point.

Eventually, I spotted the bird in the cover. Likewise, he eventually spotted either me, Rebel, or both and went off at a high-
speed low crawl that would have done one of his wild cousins
proud. Reb, although used to that kind of behavior from exposure to a lot of birds, was never able to relocate that sneaky
ringneck.

A couple of years ago, the DNR ran a pilot hunter safety program at Arrowhead, in which they picked up the cost of two
released pheasants for each student. I enrolled my son Matt, both
because he needed his safety certification and because I thought
it would be a great opportunity for photos and a magazine story.

At first, Dan and his helpers tried working the pheasant hunt
portion of the class just like they would for a bird-hunting client.
They stocked the bird field with four birds. Dan released one of
his fine English setters, and I turned Heidi loose. Of the four released birds, one presented itself for a shot by a student. We spotted another as it flushed through some evergreens below the
field. The other two ran or flew off the area before the young
hunters got anywhere near them.

On that particular day, the birds were behaving in such a
way that we finally resorted to "setting up" the situations for the
kids. We'd hold the dogs while the birds were planted some 50
yards in front of us. Then we'd turn them loose while coach and
young student walked up to a dog on point—often a considerable
distance from where the bird started.

Perhaps the best example of the problems presented by preserve pheasants can be derived from the numerous "pheasant
championships" held on these establishments (more on the contests themselves later).

One hundred fifty teams participated in the U.S. Open in
April 1987 at the Minnesota Horse and Hunt Club near Min-
neapolis. These teams, consisting of two hunters and a dog, are
made up primarily of participants, both human and canine, who
are very experienced pheasant hunters. Of the 150 teams, fewer
than 40 managed to bag their goal of six birds, and only 3 teams
killed the limit with six shells. If preserve birds were that easy,
there would have been a much higher percentage coming in with
six birds and a lot fewer birds missed.

The pheasant is a bird which takes very well to preserve life.
Once released, as you can see from the above examples, they
often display the same bag of tricks used by their wild cousins.
While stocking such released birds has been shown to have almost no beneficial results on wild bird numbers, because the
birds are not that well equipped to survive natural enemies and
weather, they can do a pretty good job of eluding two-legged
predators.

Having said all of that, I must now admit that I don't really
like preserve pheasants. While I don't want to pay to shoot sitting
ducks, I would at least like a chance at some return on the bucks
I shell out for released birds. All too often, pheasants simply
refuse to cooperate.

That doesn't mean that I don't hunt preserves. In fact, I
make at least a couple of trips per season, usually more. But I
seldom hunt preserve pheasants. Normally, I'll opt for quail or
chukar partridge. I hunt preserves to get some shooting and to
sharpen my dogs. Both quail and chukar hold nicely for points
and usually have the decency to offer reasonable shots. Preserve
pheasants sometimes don't offer any shot at all and far too often
lead my dogs on the kind of chases they get enough of while
hunting wild birds.

Another reason I prefer chukar and quail is purely economic.
You can usually buy about three quail for the price of one
pheasant, or three chukar for the price of two ringnecks. When
you add the risk of pheasants running or flying off before you get
there, quail and chukar make even more sense from a fiscal
standpoint.

The Conservation Reserve Program has also done a lot to
increase the number of preserves in many areas. The only money
farmers can make from CRP ground, other than their govern-

ment payments, is from recreation such as hunting or fishing. With the excellent cover, bird hunting is a natural. So the farmer invests in some pen-raised birds, and another preserve is born.

The problem is that many farmers don't realize what they are getting into. The federal government is quick to tell them that they can charge for hunting, but not so quick to point out that they may be opening themselves to all sorts of liability problems unless they have the proper insurance coverage. The law in many states specifies that there is no liability if landowners simply grant access for free. However, once they start to turn a buck off hunting, the situation changes.

The same holds true for lease agreements between a hunter or a group of hunters and a landowner. Some writers, seeing the growth in popularity of big game leases (including quail leases in places like Texas and waterfowl leases in other areas), see this as the future of upland hunting in general and pheasant hunting in particular.

I can't see it happening to pheasant hunting. Big game leases work because of the perceived value of a trophy deer, bear, or whatever. Waterfowl leases work because a fresh supply of birds is just over the horizon. Texas quail leases work because, even at fifty cents to one dollar per acre, a rancher can turn enough profit on a 10,000-acre spread to afford insurance coverage. In most parts of the pheasant range, a 1,000-acre farm is pretty big. Even with that amount of land, unless he or she is able to get an exorbitant amount of money per acre, a farmer can't afford to buy the insurance protection that is needed.

But there are some farmers around who don't realize the liability problem and don't know that they are literally betting the farm in order to make enough money to buy Christmas presents. And there are plenty of hunters around with more than enough money to entice landowners to lease their land. Fortunately for the rest of us, there does not seem to be enough of either group to make a significant dent in the amount of land open to those who make a polite request for permission.

Depending on where you happen to go, other types of fee hunting may prevail. In the traditional best pheasant range of South Dakota, it is very difficult to hunt for free. Most landowners charge so much per hunter per day, and in that famous pheasant state, the market seems to bear it. Other farmers and ranchers offer a combination pheasant hunt/bed-and-breakfast or bed-and-all-three-meals operation.

Combining bed-and-breakfast with pheasant hunting has

proven quite successful for a couple of enterprising Iowa farmers, Darwin Linn and Bob Manke of Corning. A few years back, they started Pheasants Galore, a company which acts as the middle-man between hunters and farmers. Pheasants Galore recruits farmers to participate, then books hunting parties for bed-and-breakfast at the farm, along with the privilege of hunting the landowner's ground. It is a pretty fair arrangement for all concerned: the hunters, who have a place to stay and hunt for about seventy-five dollars per person per day; the farmer, who has a booking agent for the hunters and who gets liability coverage from Pheasants Galore; and Pheasants Galore, which splits the profits with the farmers.

As part of my "research" on pheasant hunting (one of the benefits of being an outdoor writer with an avid interest in ringnecks), I've hunted Pheasants Galore ground on two occasions. On the first, just a one-day trip, I hunted excellent cover and shot a limit of birds. The second time around, I enjoyed bed-and-breakfast with a southwest Iowa farm family which took very good care of my nutritional needs. (In fact, it took me about all day to walk off that breakfast!) Once again, I hunted excellent cover but didn't have the opportunity to fire a single shot.

That was mid-December of 1988, when I was having great difficulty finding birds anywhere. For that reason, I was pretty understanding about that hunt. But had I come from a great distance, pounded ground for two days without seeing a rooster in range, and paid good money for it, I expect that I would have been pretty disappointed. A sure thing is awfully hard to guarantee on wild birds.

There are also all sorts of guide services available to pheasant hunters. Some will furnish everything—license, dogs, food, lodging, bird cleaning and packaging, ground transportation—and will probably charge a premium fee for it as well, perhaps ranging up to as much as several hundred dollars per hunter per day. Once more, it's a question of whatever the market will bear. If I didn't have ready access to good wild pheasant hunting, and if I had that kind of money to spend, perhaps I'd be willing to fork it over. I would certainly hope that I'd get very high-quality shooting in return.

I've only hunted with a guide once, and it wasn't because I needed help finding birds. I was doing a piece on pay pheasant hunting and had heard of a guy named Dick Bartlett out of Des Moines. We hunted southern Iowa, where Dick had access to some 9,000 acres of private ground.

Dick provided the dogs—a couple of close-working Britts—
lunch, transportation from Des Moines, and at that time (several
years ago) was charging fifty dollars per hunter per day. I had a
good, although not spectacular, hunt, shot a couple of birds, and
told him that I thought he should charge more.

I once gave some thought to entering the guiding racket myself. I'd been toying with the idea when a farmer friend approached me with a proposition to lease hunting rights on his
land. Since he farmed about 2,000 acres, a lot of it with good
pheasant cover, it seemed like the perfect setup.

The more I thought about it, the more doubts I began to
have. What if I booked a bunch of drunks or a careless hunter
who ended up shooting me or one of my dogs? What if they
couldn't hit the proverbial broad side of a barn and felt that half a
dozen good shots at roosters in a day wasn't worth what I was
charging? What if they weren't in shape to do the necessary
walking? What if, because of adverse weather or a scarcity of
game, I couldn't put them into birds?

Eventually, the what ifs won out. I decided not to take something I enjoy and risk turning it into something I might regret.

The way I look at fee hunting for wild birds, whether it be
with a guide or with an operation such as Pheasants Galore, is
that there will always be a market. Essentially, you are paying
someone to take some of the risk out of your pheasant hunting
trip. You may be paying for a place to hunt, for someone to help
you find the birds, or both. Theoretically, the more you pay, the
more you should reduce the risk of striking out. Of course, things
don't always work out that way. The bargain basement hunt may
prove to be a real find, but then again it may not. How happy you
are with what you get depends largely on how important the
money is to you in the first place and what it takes to satisfy you.

In 1989 writer Jim Schlender flew up from Atlanta to hunt
with me. The last day of his Iowa hunt, I arranged for my friend
Miles Tratchel of Newton to take us out. On that early December
morning, with the season five weeks old, we had our limit in
about two and a half hours—and each of us missed at least a
couple of shots.

Needless to say, we saw a lot of birds. In fact, I don't want to
estimate how many we did see, because even with my notes from
that day, I have trouble believing my memory. Jim said he'd
never seen anything like it, and Miles and I, who have both been
chasing Iowa pheasants for quite a few years, agreed that it was
an incredible hunt.

I suppose some paying customers might have been disappointed because we were done hunting well before noon. Some, assuming I had been the guide, might have insisted on shooting my limit as well as their own. You never know what it takes to satisfy some people. I guess that's why I'm glad that I never became a guide, except for free with friends.

The desire to prove who's the best shot or who owns the best dog has resulted in the development and proliferation of various types of field trials for just about all breeds of hunting dogs. It has also played a part in the numerous trap, skeet, and sporting clays tournaments. A number of shooting preserves have jumped on the bandwagon by combining both human and canine competition in pheasant hunting "championships."

The typical pheasant championship is based on teams, comprised of two hunters and a dog. A specified number of birds are released for the hunters. There is a time limit, and each hunter has a limited number of shells. The goal is to bag as many of the released birds as possible, with as few shots, within the time limit.

The usual formula is six birds released, six shells per hunter, and a half-hour time limit. I've heard of at least one championship where all three totals have been doubled.

In many cases, it takes all six birds and a time of under ten minutes to win one of these affairs. In the U.S. Open in 1987, my partner and I were six for six in twenty-three minutes, and finished eleventh in the pointing dog division, which had about seventy-five entries.

In other contests, the results are not so spectacular. The first time I ever entered one, my partner Gene Kroupa and I finished in a tie for third out of about thirty-five teams and bagged only five of the six birds. Actually, we had a lock on second place, but I missed one bird with both barrels. Gene has never let me live that one down.

Some of the contests divide the pointing and flushing breeds into two divisions. Some award points for dog work, although even if the dog is given a score, it is only a minor part of the total.

In all cases of which I am aware, a judge accompanies the team. His function is to make sure that the rules are followed and to verify the time. One nearly universal rule is that the birds must be shot in the air. In some contests, a bird caught by your dog counts as a bird in the bag, but you have to give up a shell. In others, all birds must be shot by the contestants in order to count. This can be tough in some cases, because preserve pheasants may sit overly tight in heavy cover, and dogs used to working wild birds may not give them the benefit of the doubt if they don't get airborne quickly enough.

Strategy plays an important part in these contests. One of the rules at the U.S. Open was that the birds had to be shot within specified boundaries, marked with blaze orange tape. Worried that my pointer might go off the area in pursuit of a runner, I convinced my partner, Dave Prine, that we should work the perimeter of the bird field first. We did, and it was a waste of time. All the birds were in the middle of the field, fairly close to where they had been released from the stocking vehicle.

In fact, working the cover adjacent to the road used by the bird planters is almost always the best procedure to follow. Arrowhead's Dan Mullin, who manages the longest-running championship I'm aware of, and who has been a participant in several other contests, verifies this. "Go after the easy birds first, and worry about the hard ones later," he says.

Speed is obviously a key ingredient in these affairs. I entered two of them with Jake, and another with Rebel. In all three cases, we had ample time within the given half hour to cover the entire bird field at least twice. Although the fields differ in size, I'd guess that 20 acres, almost all in very good cover, is about average.

In all three cases, my team found at least six birds. I think we were lucky, because we never really had a problem with running pheasants. In fact, the reason good dog work was so vital was because the birds didn't move a lot. The dog had to cover a lot of ground in order to get within scenting distance of the birds.

Luck is definitely a factor in these contests. There are usually at least two bird fields, and for various reasons, one may be easier than the other. Because the contests usually run on at least two days, weather may also change, putting some teams at a distinct advantage (or disadvantage), depending on when they hunt.

The success of the preceding team is another critical factor. If they only find two or three birds, that may mean they have left some of their six, in addition to the birds which are stocked for you. This bird buildup can make a real difference. To offset the advantage of teams running later in the day, when there is likely to be some buildup, most preserves stock a couple of extra birds for the first team's hunt.

However, the only really bad experience I had in a championship came when things should have been in our favor. The team ahead of us had only moved two birds. Our results showed that clearly—Jake found something like eleven or twelve pheasants.

Poor shooting, a couple of birds that sat too long and got caught by the dog (they had to be shot in this competition), and a couple of others that had to be chased to fly, made it a real circus. It was all topped off when my partner forgot to chamber a shell in his pump, costing us what should have been the easiest bird of the day.

Do these contests really show who the best pheasant hunters are? Not really. Although they are just about always won by good shots with good dogs, and although the simulation of a pheasant hunt is about as good as it can be in an artificial situation, it isn't quite like the real thing.

In my opinion, the best pheasant hunter is someone who studies natural cover, knows where to find the birds, is a crack shot, and has a super dog. I'd like to locate a dozen people like that, put them down in an area where there are a lot of wild birds and a lot of excellent cover, and let them go at it. Ideally, they would be able to look the cover over, select their preferred piece of ground, and hunt it. It would be something more akin to a bass tournament.

Unfortunately, hunting doesn't work that way. You'd probably end up with several hunters wanting to work the same area, which, unlike in fishing, is not very practical. You'd probably have to draw for choice of cover, which would inject the element of luck, just like in the preserve contests.

Besides, wild bird hunting is not a competitive sport, at least not for this hunter. Sure, I've had years when I've averaged a pheasant in the bag in under two hours of hunting time, working all sorts of cover, at all times of the year, and in all kinds of weather conditions. But I'm not out there to establish any kind of record. I'm there to enjoy the experience, to applaud my dogs' points, and to marvel at their retrieves. I'm not racing anyone, not even myself. Nor do I want to, because that would take most of the fun out of it. I keep records of such things as time afield, points, and birds killed simply to remind myself of past experiences and to compare pheasant hunting from season to season.

For that reason, I guess the contests are better left to the preserves. I've enjoyed them after the season is over, although I must admit that I'd rather do my preserve hunting in a more relaxed manner, where I can enjoy the dog work and the shooting without the pressure of competition. Others, who are of a more competitive nature, may find the contests more their cup of tea.

Although I think the shooting preserve business will continue to grow, I do not foresee an explosion in the popularity of pay pheasant hunting in general. I've already indicated one reason, which is that it just isn't all that much of an economic benefit to the farmer, especially not if it means a liability risk.

But the CRP is the main reason why I don't see a lot of fee hunting in the future. With millions of acres enrolled in the heart of pheasant country, bird numbers are up. There are simply more good places to hunt pheasants. As long as the CRP is with us, I expect this situation to prevail. And with that amount of good hunting available for the asking, I just can't see many pheasant hunters laying out lots of money to hunt.

Those who want to pay, however, will certainly have their options. I see nothing wrong with that, as long as it does not squeeze out those who can't pay. Hunting is an American tradition, and I'd hate to see this nation give up that heritage to become another Europe. Every time I thank a farmer or drop off a dressed bird with a landowner's wife, I try to remind myself how lucky we are to have so much excellent hunting, all free for the asking.

Pheasants Forever

N this final chapter, I'll take a look at the future of pheasant hunting. Not coincidentally, the chapter's title also happens to be the name of a national organization, Pheasants Forever, whose goal is to improve pheasant populations through habitat protection and restoration. I'll examine Pheasants Forever and what it has accomplished in the few years since it was founded.

To make any kind of accurate prediction about the future of the pheasant, we have to look at the past. If we can determine when and why the birds prospered, and when and why they declined, we can then make an educated guess as to what the future holds.

The reasons for highs and lows in pheasant populations vary from region to region. I want to emphasize here that I intend to focus on the situation in the area I know best—the Midwest and, specifically, Iowa. While there are certainly some similarities between the Midwest and other areas with well-established bird populations, such as the East or the Northwest, there are undoubtedly important differences as well.

However, the major factor in maintaining good bird populations everywhere is the availability of the proper habitat. Although significant changes in bird numbers from one year to the next may occur because of weather factors, such as a very severe winter or a particularly cold, wet nesting season, over the long term the birds will recover if they have the right habitat.

In the Midwest, pheasant numbers tended to remain quite high during periods of agricultural diversity. Most of us in this part of the country can remember when the average farm was about 200–300 acres. The typical farmer had some livestock—probably at least a few cows and pigs, along with a flock of barnyard chickens—and a number of small fields planted in different crops. You were very likely to find oats and alfalfa, in addition to corn and soybeans, all on the same small farm, and probably no field larger than 40 acres.

That situation changed very gradually. Livestock operations have grown much larger, and farmers tend to specialize in either cattle or hogs. Many landowners have no livestock at all and plant everything they can in row crops.

The Soil Bank, a popular long-term set-aside program, ended in the early 1960s. That change, on top of what had already happened in agriculture, took away much of the remaining nesting and winter cover. Farmers had already removed numerous fencerows and had planted more and more acres in row crops. When the federal program was ended, pheasants lost many large blocks of cover, places where they had reproduced and found refuge from the weather for years.

Because the changes were gradual, and because the pheasant is a hardy, adaptable bird, there were no immediate, drastic declines in bird numbers. But following a hard winter or two, or a poor nesting season, numbers tumbled. Unlike the past, when plenty of good habitat was available, the birds no longer recovered even when nesting and wintering conditions were favorable.

In some states, the bottom really dropped out. Formerly good pheasant states, such as Michigan and Ohio, saw their pheasant hunting plummet to lows they never would have expected, even in their worst nightmares. In Minnesota, the yearly bird harvest went from close to a million in the early 1960s to one-third of that by 1980.

Comparatively speaking, the "Big Four" of pheasant hunting—South Dakota, Nebraska, Kansas, and Iowa—never had it as bad as most of the rest of the pheasant range. But even in the ringneck's stronghold, drastic changes were occurring.

In 1963 pheasant hunters in Iowa bagged nearly 2 million birds. In 1965, following a severe blizzard on St. Patrick's Day which killed thousands of birds in northern Iowa, the daily limit was reduced to 2 pheasants. The total bird harvest dropped by some 800,000.

For the next fifteen years, the bird harvest stayed relatively stable, varying from 1.2 to 1.8 million in most seasons. The 1973 harvest, at 1.9 million, wasn't much different from what it had been a decade earlier.

Then, in the 1980s, things began to change for the worse. The 1982 harvest dropped below a million for the first time since records had been kept. In 1983 the Payment in Kind (PIK) program took millions of acres out of production for one year and brought about a short-term resurgence. But the 1984 harvest of 724,000, the worst on record, showed that there was definitely something wrong.

What had happened was that Iowa was finally paying for those changes in habitat. Why had it taken so long for things to bottom out? Mainly because the state had enjoyed relatively mild winters and fairly favorable nesting conditions. The early 1980s brought a succession of severe winters. Where the birds couldn't find adequate shelter, they died.

Northern Iowa, which once had boasted the state's best pheasant hunting, suffered the most. The winters are harsher there, and the birds' need for shelter more critical. Much of that part of Iowa is quite flat, and it is the state's most intensively farmed region. That combination of factors dealt the pheasant population a near fatal blow. Things couldn't have looked much worse for the Midwest's favorite game bird.

But by 1987, just three years later, the pheasant harvest had doubled. Many people, myself included, were fully expecting Iowa hunters to harvest close to two million birds per season at some point in the early 1990s. What made the difference?

There are two answers, one long-term and one short-term. The long-term answer is habitat, the same factor which had changed so gradually but which had kept Iowa bird numbers from recovering from the lows of the early 1980s. The short-term answer is weather, which had caused those dramatic declines from one year to the next.

The last long, hard winter of the decade occurred in 1985. That is also the last year Iowa was hit by a killer storm. Following a Thanksgiving weekend blizzard, when the windchill factor dropped to below −60 degrees, I found numerous birds frozen solid. And this was in a part of the state with plenty of good cover. I can't imagine what happened where there was little or no winter shelter.

The winter of 1985 was followed by a succession of mild winters. These happened to coincide with the passage of the 1985 Farm Bill, which included the Conservation Reserve Program (CRP). The CRP established an attractive ten-year set-aside program for farmers. With corn and soybean prices remaining low, many landowners were quick to enroll in the CRP.

Almost all CRP ground provides excellent nesting habitat, and much of it is good winter cover as well. The pheasant population in Iowa has recovered dramatically. The only question now is whether there might be problems just around the corner.

With the possible exception of the bobwhite quail, no other popular game bird is as closely tied to agriculture as is the pheasant. The ringneck's fate hinges directly upon whatever direction farming takes. As we approach the end of the twentieth century, there are so many forces exerting pressure on agriculture that it is truly mind-boggling.

The days when a farmer planted crops and raised livestock based solely on the need for economic survival and the preservation of land are gone forever. It is not uncommon for modern farmers to make more money in government subsidies than they do from selling what they produce. Washington keeps commodity prices artificially low to protect consumers. At the same time, our government encourages the highest possible crop yields by basing its subsidy payments on what the farmer has produced over a given period of time.

These policies encourage farmers to get the maximum amount of production out of those fields which are planted in crops. This in turn results in the use of all available modern technology, including herbicides and pesticides.

But the general public is also expressing legitimate concerns about water and air quality. The government is attempting to respond to these concerns and to worries that overly intensive crop production is resulting in excessive losses of irreplaceable topsoil through erosion.

The result is a national "farm policy" which seems to make little sense to anyone. The federal government warns about the hazards of smoking yet subsidizes the production of tobacco. It indirectly encourages overproduction of such commodities as corn and then pays farmers to take land out of production in order to avoid surpluses.

Although the overall policy seldom seems to make much sense, bits and pieces of it do. The CRP is one such component. It takes erodible land out of crop production. The program reduces both soil erosion and surplus commodity production, thus killing two birds with one stone. It also rewards farmers by paying them an annual per acre subsidy for this set-aside ground.

As we have seen previously, pheasants end up being big winners in this program. The dramatic upsurge in bird numbers in the Midwest is directly attributable to the CRP. Take away the program and things could easily return to where they were in the early 1980s.

Fortunately, because this aspect of the farm program works very well both for farmers and for Washington, the CRP is not likely to be abolished in the near future.

It takes a program of this scale, with millions of acres taken out of crop production and planted to good habitat, to impact bird numbers in a big way. Most pheasants live most of their lives on or near farms. What happens on those farms determines what happens to the birds.

We pheasant hunters are fortunate beneficiaries of this program. There is no way that the individual states or private groups, even working together, could have that kind of impact. When you figure that many Iowa farmers are being paid over one hundred dollars per acre per year for their CRP ground, and that well over a million acres of Iowa farmland is enrolled, you begin to see the scope of the problem.

Farmland is too expensive to buy, or even to lease on a large enough scale, for anyone but Uncle Sam to operate a program even a fraction the size of the CRP.

I asked Richard Bishop, chief of the wildlife bureau of the Iowa Department of Natural Resources (DNR), to comment on the CRP and its effects on pheasant numbers (Rich, coincidentally, is an avid pheasant hunter himself).

> I hope Congress continues the program, and I think they will. If they do, I think that more and more land will go into the program. . . . But even the CRP isn't without its drawbacks. In some parts of southern Iowa, which used to be our best pheasant range, we probably have more land out of crop production than we need. . . . Too much grass and no food can be a problem. We really don't think that it has impacted our bird numbers that much, but what you want ideally is a good mix between nesting and winter cover and food. . . . Up in northern Iowa, we have the opposite problem. We still don't have enough cover in some of those areas that are very intensively farmed. The result is that a tough winter can really hurt the birds.

Thus, while the CRP is of overall benefit to pheasants, it is not a perfect solution. Where the terrain is rough, much of the land is considered erodible and therefore eligible for enrollment in the CRP. Flatter areas, which are often the most intensively farmed, are less likely to be considered erodible and therefore may not be eligible for the program. It can become a case of too much CRP ground in certain areas, but not enough in others.

Also, as in any government program, there are certain inequities. One of my farmer friends wanted to put an entire 350-acre farm into CRP. I had hunted that land many times, clambering up and down hills and gullies. I figured that if any ground qualified for the program, his had to.

However, the soil conservation agents rejected it. It was not erodible, they told him, because of all the terraces he had built! Meanwhile, farms all around him on which the owners had done little or nothing on their own to prevent erosion were being accepted into the CRP. Although his farm was accepted a couple of years later, it is easy to understand how many farmers get the idea that it is a case of Washington giving the biggest rewards to the least conservation-minded landowners.

Bishop also sees another key to the direction of farm policy in the future.

> People are starting to get very concerned about water quality, and I think it's going to be the key to conservation efforts in many areas. Water quality hits people where they live. You start talking about how we farm having an impact on our health, and you get people's attention. . . . I look for future legislation to deal with filter strips along streams and with the control of agricultural runoff. Just like with the CRP, wildlife may be a very minor consideration to the people in Washington when they look at water quality. But like the CRP, efforts to improve water quality are going to benefit wildlife significantly. . . . I'm very positive about the future of pheasants in the Midwest. The long-term outlook for the birds is excellent. In the short term, there are still a lot of areas with insufficient cover where weather can have a big impact.

In summary, what Washington is doing with its farm policy is good for the birds and, if anything, is likely to get better in the future.

At the same time, we should also recognize the efforts of those farmers who are doing their bit for conservation and for wildlife, and probably would regardless of federal programs.

Many of these farmers hunt themselves. Others, while not hunters, enjoy wildlife and recognize that good conservation

Farmer-hunter Jim Cuddeback of Washington, Iowa, and some of the excellent habitat he has established for pheasants.

practices are also in their own long-term interest. If you intend to stay on the land, and if your livelihood depends on it, you have to protect it.

I hunted with two such farmers in 1989. Kenneth and Jim Cuddeback are a father and son team who work together and hunt together. They enjoy pursuing deer in addition to pheasants and rabbits, and they were proud to show me the cover available to wildlife on their farms.

While much of what they did was being subsidized by Washington in the form of CRP payments, there were the small touches which showed their strong interest in wildlife. Jim had planted some small plots of grain sorghum directly adjacent to the CRP acres. Sorghum is an excellent source of high-energy winter food for pheasants.

What the Cuddebacks were doing on their own is similar to the farming practices that Pheasants Forever is encouraging in its programs. That brings us full circle to this dynamic organization of people concerned about pheasants, most of them hunters, and the story of what they have accomplished in the short time since the group was founded.

I am proud to say that Pheasants Forever (PF) got its start through the efforts of an outdoor writer. Dennis Anderson, then outdoor writer for the *St. Paul Pioneer Press and Dispatch,* wrote an article in 1981 addressing the plight of the pheasant in Minnesota, where bird numbers had plummeted. Anderson suggested creating an organization to aid pheasants, much as Ducks Unlimited had responded to the waterfowl crisis of the 1930s.

Anderson's idea received overwhelming response, and Pheasants Forever was born.

The first Pheasants Forever chapter was formed in 1983, and the organization had almost an immediate impact in the state of Minnesota. That state passed a bill requiring a five dollar pheasant stamp the same year, generating half a million dollars annually to aid in pheasant restoration.

By June 1989, Pheasants Forever had grown to well over three hundred chapters and forty-six thousand members nationally. Pheasant hunters responded to the organization even in states with good bird numbers. Iowa, for example, with a population of about three million, has more pheasants than people. Yet in its ninety-nine counties, there are ninety-one PF chapters and over fifteen thousand members.

Superficially, Pheasants Forever resembles other conservation organizations like Ducks Unlimited (DU) and The Ruffed Grouse Society (RGS). The group raises most of its money through annual banquets, just like DU and the RGS. However, there is one important difference. With the exception of membership dues, all money raised is retained by the local chapter for local projects. Pheasants Forever impacts habitat right in the backyard of its members.

Although the group focuses on local projects, it does not operate in a vacuum. Recognizing the benefits of the CRP, Pheasants Forever works with farmers to create the best possible set-aside habitat for pheasants. This includes paying the farmers to establish switchgrass, probably the best cover of all the prairie grasses. The farmer receives money from PF to do this in addition to CRP payments from Washington.

On annual set-aside (ACR) acres, PF pays farmers to leave brome/alfalfa cover undisturbed for three successive years. This cover provides additional nesting habitat for the birds.

In many areas, especially those vulnerable to severe winters, a lack of trees can be a problem for bird survival. Shelterbelts, where many birds used to sit out the worst of the blizzards, have been ripped out. Pheasants Forever is working to restore this valuable cover.

Here again, there are also state and federal government programs available to the landowner. But by combining their money and effort with government programs, PF can make shelterbelt plantings that much more attractive to the farmer.

Food plots are also important, especially in close proximity to shelter in those areas where winter cover is in short supply. Here again, PF works with state agencies. The Iowa DNR is also encouraging shelterbelt restoration and the establishment of nearby food plots in the northern half of the state. Pheasants Forever is doing the same thing and is donating corn, sorghum, and wheat to plant in the food plots.

In Iowa and Minnesota, PF works with the DNR on land acquisition projects. Nationwide, PF has purchased over 4,000 acres of land. In Iowa alone, PF chapters have combined their efforts with other organizations such as the DNR, county conservation boards, Ducks Unlimited, and the Nature Conservancy in the acquisition of 2,500 acres of land.

While these totals may not sound large, readers should consider the fact that land acquisition is an expensive proposition. Even though the total acreage may not be large, this is land which is permanently retired and protected for wildlife. It will not be impacted by the changing winds of farm policy in Washington.

Pheasants Forever has also purchased or cost-shared the acquisition of conservation equipment, such as grass drills, seeders, root plows, tractors, tree planters, etc. The chapters themselves may furnish labor to establish habitat plantings, may pay the farmers to do it, or may hire the work done through private or governmental agencies.

In addition, PF undertakes educational programs, provides funds for pheasant research, and lobbies for legislation which will benefit wildlife in general and pheasants in particular.

Typical habitat projects include planting woody cover for windbreaks or shelterbelts, sowing nesting cover, creating food plots near wintering areas, or establishing 10-acre plots which combine winter cover and food.

In the relatively short period since the group was founded, Pheasants Forever has had a significant impact on habitat. It has established nearly 160,000 acres of food plots, 9,000 acres of woody cover, and over 75,000 acres of nesting cover.

Jeff Finden, the organization's executive director, has even more ambitious ideas for the future. "Our ten year goal is to impact at least one million acres of land for pheasants," he states.

Just a few years ago, no one could have imagined that a private organization could have that kind of influence on pheasant habitat. What it has taken is an awareness that the birds were in trouble and a willingness to do something about it.

The danger is that pheasant hunters might look at the big federal programs, such as the CRP, and think that their efforts are no longer necessary. This has not happened. Pheasants Forever has continued to grow and is combining its efforts with state and federal agencies to get "the most bang for the buck."

In summary, the future of the ringneck pheasant, at least in the heart of its range across the Midwest, looks better than anyone would have imagined back in the early 1980s. While large-scale federal programs have had the most impact, the contribution made by the states, by Pheasants Forever, and by individual landowners cannot be overlooked.

Now that bird numbers are back up, we want to make sure that they stay there and even increase. There are many places across the country, and even here in the Midwest, where much more can be done for the birds. Because most pheasants live on private land, the trick is to develop programs which are beneficial both to wildlife and to the landowner. These are the only ones which are likely to meet with widespread acceptance.

As we head into the twenty-first century, we must also think of the future of the pheasant hunter. Hunting itself is under attack in many parts of the country. Young people today have many more recreational opportunities from which to choose than did those of us who became hunters a generation ago. Without some effort on the part of those of us who hunt today, there are likely to be a lot fewer hunters in the future. The dual threat of an increase in the number of antihunters and a decrease in the number of new hunters does not bode well for our sport.

But putting legions of hunters into the field is not the answer either. We must teach the new generation, and we must do it better than we ourselves were taught. Illegal and unsportsmanlike practices, which were commonplace and for the most part overlooked in the past, cannot be tolerated in the future. We no longer live in a world where everyone either hunts or doesn't hunt. We now face a situation where many of those who don't hunt are openly hostile to those of us who do.

The future of pheasant hunting is with the next generation. Here a teenage girl gets her introduction to the sport as part of an Iowa hunter safety class.

In other words, we have to clean up our own act. There is a ground swell of environmental activism in this country, and we must make sure that pheasant hunters are a part of it. When we champion sound conservation practices, through groups such as Pheasants Forever, even the nonhunting environmentalists begin to see us as part of the solution rather than as part of the problem. We must establish common ground with all environmentally concerned groups, not just with other hunters. We must work with the hikers and the bird-watchers. In so doing, we can isolate the radical antihunters and thwart their efforts.

From the vantage point of the present, the future looks very bright. The pheasant hunters of the next century have challenges to face, mostly as a result of a rapidly changing world and society. But with dedication, and with the support of organizations like Pheasants Forever, they can make that group's name more than just a title. May there be pheasants forever, as long as there are hunters who are worthy of them.

May there be pheasants forever, as long as there are hunters who are worthy of them.

Annotated Bibliography

The following is a very brief list of books that I've found either extremely informative, or enjoyable, or both. They cover not only pheasant hunting but also dogs, guns, and upland shooting in general.

Bell, Bob. *Hunting the Long-Tailed Bird.* Freshet Press, 1975. Bob Bell is a Pennsylvanian who did a lot of pheasant hunting back when gunners in that state were taking over a million birds a year. He's a no-nonsense kind of writer, and even though his book has been around for fifteen years, it's still fine reading. I owe a lot of my own thinking on the relationship of gun, choke, and load to what Bell has to say.

Brister, Bob. *Shotgunning: The Art and the Science.* Winchester Press, 1976. This book is, in my opinion, *the* modern classic on all aspects of shotgunning. Whether you are an upland or waterfowl hunter, clay target or live bird shooter, you can learn a lot by reading Brister. His studies on the effect of shot string, during which he fired at moving targets towed by his wife in the family car, are especially interesting. Brister remains one of the top gun writers to this day and is the shooting editor of *Field & Stream.* I'd like to see him update this book to deal with advances in shotshell manufacturing, especially in the area of steel shot, which have taken place since its publication. But even without revision, it still stands as the most complete and scientific look at modern shotgunning.

Duffey, David Michael. *Hunting Dog Know-How.* Winchester Press, 1965. Revised 1972. Duffey is my favorite dog trainer/writer, and this is an excellent basic book for those who are interested in acquiring and training a pheasant dog. His training advice is simple and practical, and his knowledge of the various breeds is impressive. Duffey continues to write regularly for *Gun Dog* magazine.

197

Evans, George Bird. *The Upland Shooting Life.* Alfred A. Knopf, 1971. Although this book has nothing to do with pheasant hunting, except on preserves, it had such an influence on me and my own hunting attitudes and ethics that I have to include it. I doubt that I ever would have become a grouse and woodcock hunter, and perhaps not an outdoor writer either, had I not read this book. Evans's book is an homage to the sport of wing shooting and should be read by every serious upland hunter.

Farris, Allen, Eugene Klonglan, and Richard Nomsen. *The Ring-Necked Pheasant in Iowa.* Iowa Conservation Commission, 1977. This book provides an extremely interesting history of the pheasant in Iowa. In addition, it clearly shows the effects of habitat (or a lack thereof) on pheasant populations. Written by biologists for hunters (or anyone else with a layman's interest in the birds), it is a book which is full of excellent background information on pheasants.

Grooms, Steve. *Modern Pheasant Hunting.* Stackpole Books, 1982. Steve Grooms is probably as experienced and as widely traveled a pheasant hunter as you're likely to meet. He grew up in Iowa and moved to Minnesota after college, but he still has the good sense to come back here, and to visit South Dakota quite often, for his bird hunting. Steve and I have hunted together a number of times over the past ten years, and outside of his attraction for swamp-dwelling roosters and his preference for an over-and-under, he is relatively sane as pheasant fanatics go. His book is practical, informative, and pleasant reading, and he's even included a couple of photos of me—although I've tried not to let that influence my recommendation.

Norris, Dr. Charles C. *Eastern Upland Shooting.* Countrysport Press, 1989. Despite the recent date of this book's publication, it is the oldest work in this group. It was originally published in 1946, and outside of a foreword by George Bird Evans, the new edition is a reprint of the old. Dr. Norris hunted pheasants extensively in the East, from their introduction up to the 1950s. This book captures some of the nostalgia of those times. Even though the book is nearly half a century old, much of Dr. Norris's advice still makes good sense for today's pheasant hunters.

Vance, Joel. *Upland Bird Hunting.* Outdoor Life Books, 1981. Not as widely traveled as Charles Waterman, Vance has a lot of bird-hunting experience, especially in the Midwest and on the prairies. He doesn't cover all the upland birds, which gives him more time (three chapters, in fact) to spend on pheasants. I'm almost sure that the bobwhite quail is his favorite bird, but it would probably be mine as well if I hailed from Missouri. Even with that preference, along with his opinion that most other bird dogs aren't fit to lick a Brittany's paws, Vance is still worth reading. For one thing, he has the good sense to prefer side-by-side doubles over superposeds and repeaters. Obviously, he can't be all bad.

Waterman, Charles. *Hunting Upland Birds*. Winchester Press, 1972. Waterman is like Tom Huggler in the diversity of upland hunting he has experienced, but a generation older. He has hunted every upland bird on the North American continent and covers all of them in this book. Appropriately enough, there is a long chapter devoted to pheasants. Once you read what Waterman has to say about ringnecks, you'll find that you want to read what he has to say about all the other birds as well. His writing grows on you.